The Bible in the Pulpit

The Bible in the Pulpit

The Renewal of Biblical Preaching

Leander E. Keck

Abingdon   Nashville

THE BIBLE IN THE PULPIT

Library of Congress Cataloging in Publication Data

Keck, Leander E
  The Bible in the pulpit.

   1.   Bible—Homiletical use—Addresses, essays,
lectures. 2.   Preaching—Addresses, essays, lectures.
3. Sermons, American. I. Title.
BS534.5.K42   251'.08   77-12015

ISBN 0-687-03160-5

MANUFACTURED BY THE PARTHENON PRESS AT
NASHVILLE, TENNESSEE, UNITED STATES OF AMERICA

Contents

Preface

Effective biblical preaching is an art as well as a skill. The more I have pondered the matter, the more convinced I have become that it is an art that needs to be recovered. I have also become ever more persuaded that what is needed is not so much guidelines for the step-by-step preparation of sermons as a perspective within which such guidelines have meaning, a conceptual framework that might clarify the task as a whole. I am also convinced that precisely for biblical preaching, those of us who are professional students of the Bible in theological seminaries have a responsibility to clarify for preaching the significance of what we do. This book is a modest attempt to make such a contribution.

I am deeply aware of the many limitations of this book, of the numerous aspects of the matter that are either mentioned only in passing or bypassed altogether. Because preaching is an event in which the Christian faith becomes articulate, there is scarcely an aspect of theology—broadly conceived—that does not come to bear on the task. Nonetheless it has been necessary to be selective. By design, I have tried to write simply and directly, keeping as far as possible to the style of oral presentation that played an important role in the development of the material.

This book is a progress report. It puts into print an approach to biblical preaching that has been in the making for some years. It began as the H. I. Hester Lectures given at

Midwestern Baptist Theological Seminary in Kansas City in the spring of 1973. I want to express once more my sincere appreciation to that seminary community for providing the stimulus to focus ideas that had been developing for some time. Parts of chapter 3 were put to paper in connection with the Bailey Lectures at Berkeley Baptist Divinity School given in May, 1969; as the book developed, the material has been shared with ministers' conferences, pastors' schools, and continuing education seminars at Candler. Each of these occasions provided opportunity for conversations that contributed significantly to the clarification of the issues. During a sabbatical in Cambridge, England, in 1976, facilitated by the Association of Theological Schools, I rewrote the first two chapters completely. Colleagues—pastors and professors—have read the manuscript at various stages. For all these occasions and modes of assistance I am deeply grateful.

LEANDER E. KECK

The Bible in the Pulpit

Chapter One

On the Malaise
of Biblical Preaching

Every renewal of Christianity has been accompanied by a renewal of preaching. Each renewal of preaching, in turn, has rediscovered biblical preaching. Nineteen centuries of experience suggests clearly that unless there is a recovery of biblical preaching, the dissipation of the Christian faith will continue.

To be sure, "conservative churches are growing," and their appeal is in part attributable to their claim that they "preach the Bible."[1] Whether their mode of doing so is actually biblical is another matter, as we shall see. Right at the outset, however, it must be emphasized that it is far easier to preach the Bible unbiblically than to do so biblically. What makes preaching "biblical" is what a good deal of this book is about.

The Bible itself determines when preaching is biblical, just as it is Mozart who determines when music is Mozartean. But what is the Bible? That question is not simply rhetorical, it is crucial—precisely because the answer is not obvious. The demise of biblical preaching in many Protestant churches is partly traceable to confusion at just this point. This confusion reflects the fact that the Bible has become a different book for us. This is not because the King James Version or the Douay Version has been replaced by contemporary translations, and certainly not because the content has been changed. Rather, the Bible has become a different book for us because our thinking has been historicized. That is, we take for granted that to understand something one should see it in its historical setting. This is as true of art, social institutions, or ideas as it is of literature.

Historical thinking means perceiving things in historical relationships, as part of the stream of events and factors that conditions everything. Historical thinking understands things in light of continuities and developments, antecedents and consequences, contexts and contingencies. Increasingly for the past two centuries the Bible has come to be understood as a historical book, not simply because much of it is concerned with history, but above all because every aspect of it and everything in it is conditioned by history. To the extent that this is acknowledged, the Bible becomes a different book for us from what it was for Martin Luther, the Council of Trent, or John Wesley.

If the Bible determines when preaching is biblical, and if the Bible has come to be a different book because we understand it historically, then the criterion of biblical preaching is historicized as well. It is no longer the amount of the Bible cited that makes preaching biblical. The impact of historical thinking across the board, and with regard to the Bible in particular, has made the appeal to Scripture more complex and more subtle.

The most direct effect of historical thinking on the Bible has come by way of biblical criticism as it developed since the eighteenth century. Apart from outright fundamentalist circles, Catholic no less than Protestant, some form of biblical criticism, and of the historical thinking that it manifests, is found today in virtually all theological seminaries. The picture is by no means uniform, as the recent controversies among Missouri Synod Lutherans show. Nonetheless, the biblical faculties in conservative evangelical seminaries participate in the same professional societies, read the same books, write for the same journals and, most important, teach the Bible with the same general critical method as those in liberal schools. In recent decades, Catholic biblical scholarship has developed remarkably, so that today no serious student of the Bible can ignore the work done by Catholic scholars. We have gotten so used to this whole development that we easily overlook its momentous character. Never before have religious communities, including Reformed and Conservative Judaism, trained their leadership by encouraging a historical, critical approach to their Scriptures. There is nothing comparable in Islam today, nor in the religions of the Far East. The impact of this phenomenon on the Bible's role in preaching, however, has been mixed indeed, and not always positive.

The Bible does not belong to the guild of professional scholars; the Bible belongs first of all to the church. To be sure, the church does not "possess" the Bible as a private treasure. Accordingly, in colleges and universities, highly important biblical study, and related research that is significant for it, is proceeding irrespective of how the results might or might not impinge on preaching. Indeed, such work would often not be undertaken by theological seminaries because its significance for professional education is too indirect. Still, there is more intensive scholarly work being done on the Bible, in and out of seminaries, today than ever before. But what is its import for preaching? In other words, if the Bible determines when preaching is biblical we must bring to bear what we have come to know about the Bible as the result of this intensive scholarly effort. It is appropriate for biblical scholarship to throw its understanding of the matter onto the scale and to draw the consequences of its work for preaching. There is no reason why the matter should be left entirely in the hands of others.

This book, then, is the attempt by a New Testament student to bring into focus the significance of what we have come to know about the Bible, and to do so in a way that can renew biblical preaching. We may rephrase the matter: although some preachers have surmised that it was biblical criticism that led to the demise of biblical preaching, biblical criticism can provide a mode of understanding that will release the Bible into life of the church.

The central role assigned to biblical criticism here is not simply special pleading by a professor of New Testament, plaintively insisting that preachers—his former and future students—take scholarly work seriously, even less that biblical criticism is the savior of the church's preaching task. Rather, I am persuaded that communicating the import of historical understanding for preaching is an important aspect of my profession as a scholar and of my vocation as a theological educator. When a professor of New Testament writes about biblical preaching he is not dabbling in someone else's discipline (that of the homiletician), nor taking an imperious stand vis-à-vis the church. He is simply bringing one important aspect of his work to fruition where it counts most—or ought to. The rationale is not obscure: the focal point of biblical research is the exegesis of the text. The exegetical process in turn is not complete until the text is released into the present-day form of that community for which it was written in the first place.

This book is not, therefore, a manual on how to preach biblical sermons—though some suggestions will not be absent either. Nor is it a theological essay on the Word of God in the Bible and its relation to the Word in the sermon—though we shall have some observations on this matter also. The book is an attempt to state succinctly the possibility, and necessity, of preaching biblically, and of doing so in accord with the character of the Bible itself.

One might ask whether preaching of any sort has not been eroded to the point that before one can renew specifically biblical preaching one must first rehabilitate preaching in general. One could show rather easily that preaching has lost its centrality in most main-line white Protestant churches, although it has never lost its place in black Protestantism and is being rediscovered in the Catholic Church. The white Protestant pastor who still devotes a major block of his time preparing sermons—especially scholarly or biblical ones—has been on the endangered species list for a long time. Today it is administration that gets the lion's share of one's energy. What is left is apportioned to counseling and routine pastoral care, "board sitting" on community agencies; sundry matters have displaced Sunday matters. The proliferation of tasks has squeezed virtually to the vanishing point blocks of time free from interruption, time essential for sermon preparation and especially for long-range reading and reflection.

Nonetheless, the centrality of preaching is assumed here to be a given of the Christian faith; I shall not argue the case for preaching. Whoever says that preaching is passé is the one who bears the burden of proof. What is really passé, I suspect, is the point of view from which such judgments are made. The question is not, Does preaching have a future? but rather, What sort of future will preaching have? Moreover, it is not a resurgence of preaching in general—any sort of pulpit discourse that is different and interesting—that will renew biblical preaching along the way. Rather, it may well be the other way around: the renewal of biblical preaching can rejuvenate preaching in general, and thereby renew the church.

It is folly to speak of renewing the church, and particularly of renewing preaching by means of biblical preaching, if one does not think that the situation calls for it. Is the situation really so serious? Is preaching in disarray, and is biblical preaching in such neglect or disrepute? Is the state of preaching worse than that of lecturing, and do the expository sermons actually being preached bore people more than do exegetical courses? I do not claim that the situation at the podium is better than it is in the pulpit, though I would be prepared to consider that the renewal of effective lecturing might do wonders for education. There is solid and significant preaching being done in many places, and I have benefited from some of it; still, on the whole, the situation is rather bleak. This impression is the cumulation of all sorts of experience in churches and among preachers, and has usually been confirmed by them. It is useful to reflect briefly on how we got into this situation. Then we shall reflect on the consquences of being there.

Factors in the Malaise

The present state of biblical preaching, like that of preaching in general, did not spring up overnight like a mushroom, but is the result of multiple factors interacting with one another across many decades. We shall focus on three of these which have been significant in the devolution of biblical preaching: controversies over the Bible, Protestantism's confusion about the place of Scripture in the church, and the preacher's own ambivalence. Noting these will locate certain issues to be addressed in the chapters that follow.

American Protestantism has been deeply scarred by *con-*

troversies over the Bible. Two aspects, though interrelated, can be distinguished for brief comment. First, the rise of biblical criticism embroiled the churches in conflicts over the nature and authority of the Bible. Almost a century ago, C. A. Briggs at Union Theological Seminary in New York was tried for heresy. More than forty years ago, Princeton Theological Seminary was split and a rival Presbyterian seminary (Westminster) was founded. American Baptists started "conservative" seminaries in Philadelphia and Chicago to counteract the liberalism of Crozer and the University of Chicago. Fifteen years ago, Southern Baptists dismissed an Old Testament professor for writing a commentary on Genesis that worked with critical positions long accepted elsewhere. Recently the Missouri Synod's Concordia Seminary experienced such discord that the majority of the faculty and students went into "exile" on a Roman Catholic campus. Often these battles have involved congregations, not only professors and administrators. Laypersons were drawn into the fray, and sometimes led the assault troops. Bible schools and Bible colleges emerged, and publishing houses were created to promote "Bible believing" curriculum materials.

These wars over the Bible and biblical criticism have had an unfortunate impact on biblical preaching. On the one hand, many a sermon was devoted to defending a particular view of the Bible (whether orthodox or critical) instead of interpreting the content of the Bible. On the other hand, preachers who wanted to avoid controversial topics found things to preach that were not divisive, or that appealed to the Bible in a noncontroversial way. Both consequences sold the content of the Bible short, and often aborted the gospel as well.

Second, the content and import of the Bible became involved in controversies over social and moral matters.

The Bible in the Pulpit

Whether it was "temperance" (a euphemism for the prohibition movement), racial desegregation, or women's rights in and out of the church, the Bible has been quoted by all combatants. It has become a truism that "You can prove anything with the Bible." Those who agree with the preacher's views on matters of public policy or personal morality are reinforced in their conviction that they represent the biblical standpoint; those who disagree suspect that the preacher is using the Bible selectively against them, and that another preacher could refute the sermon with other passages from the same Bible. As a result, the biblical coinage has been debased; "what the Bible has to say" is of less value today than before precisely because there has been too much appeal to the Bible in some quarters—or at least too much of the wrong kind of appeal. Such a situation erodes the place of biblical preaching in general because congregations are no longer sure that they can trust the use of Scripture with regard to issues that concern them most.

In the next place, largely as a result of the rise of biblical criticism and the controversies over the Bible, there is widespread *confusion about the Bible's proper place in the life of the church*, ranging from indifference (in white, liberalized Protestant churches) to stout defense of orthodox dogmas about the Bible. True, it is difficult, and doubtless dangerous, to generalize about so diverse a phenomenon as the standing of the Bible in main-line Protestant churches today. There are many pastors who have fairly clear ideas on the subject and emphasize the Bible in the life of the church, but their congregations seem to be rather indifferent to it. A few years ago one pastor told me that less than one percent of his suburban congregation showed any interest in the possibility of a Bible study and that the majority openly discouraged him from even undertaking such a thing. Often, Bible study is a concession to pious minorities within the congregation. Congregations that regard themselves as being shaped by the Bible and as being accountable to it are rare indeed. Conversely, many a congregation has a high estimate of the Bible and wishes that its pastor shared it. Despite great diversity in this matter, James D. Smart was on target when he wrote *The Strange Silence of the Bible in the Church.*[2]

Elizabeth Achtemeier wrote trenchantly of the indifference toward the Bible:

> It is now possible in this country to carry on the expected work of a Protestant congregation with no reference to the Bible whatsoever. The worship services of the church can be divorced from Biblical models and become the celebration of the congregation's life together and of its more or less vaguely held common beliefs in some god. Folk songs, expressive of American culture, can replace the psalms of the church. Art forms and aesthetic experiences can be used as substitutes for communion with God. The preacher's opinions or ethical views can be made replacements for the word from the Biblical text. The Sacraments can be turned into expressions of simply the congregation's fellowship together. But the amazing thing is that no one in the pew on Sunday morning may notice. Indeed, such a worship service may win praise from some quarters as "contemporary" and "relevant."[3]

The confusion about the place of the Bible and the uncertainty about its authority in the church appear to prevail in those sectors of Protestantism which have been most hospitable to biblical criticism. This outcome of the many controversies is tragic, for it suggests that although the battles have been won to a considerable degree, the fruits of victory have been squandered. Instead of using freedom from dogmatism, archaism, and biblicism in order to appropriate the Bible in ways which accord with the newer insights, liberal Protestantism has turned emancipation from biblicism into freedom from the Bible as Scripture. To be sure, the Bible has seldom been rejected outright. Its place is more like that of the old grandmother who has a room in the house and who appears at meals, but who has little real influence on the life of the family. Though honored occasionally, she is a tolerated relic in the midst of deep hunger for continuity and stability.

It will repay us to clarify this loss of canonicity which the Bible has experienced in liberalized Protestantism. The Bible may still be regarded as an important resource for inspiration and ethical principles, and it can be respected as a valuable repository of early Christian beliefs or as a record of the human quest for God. But when the Bible has such a status it is no longer canon in any recognizable sense. Indeed, many Christians find the whole idea of a canon, a "closed" Scripture, to be offensive. They surmise quite rightly that many other books are available that can be used profitably by the church, and that are often far easier to understand than the Bible. Can one not be just as inspired, just as motivated, just as educated in the Christian faith through Bonhoeffer's letters as from Paul's (also from prison), or through parables and short stories more recent than those from Jesus? Are not the heroic deeds of more recent Christians as worthy of emulation as the exploits of ancient apostles and prophets? And why not use the literature of other religions as well? Is it not sheer provincialism and traditionalism to exalt the Bible in the church and pulpit? Would it not be better to have a loose-leaf Bible whose contents can be changed from generation to generation, and from community to community? Questions like these are asked repeatedly. They reveal the massive confusion over what it means for the church to have a Scripture, and over the significance of having the kind of canon it does in fact have.

On the Malaise of Biblical Preaching

Whereas liberalized Protestantism appears to have de-canonized the Bible, right-wing Protestants have over-canonized it. Here the Bible is regarded as an essentially miraculous book that by definition cannot be understood properly if one does not grant its special status at the outset. In order to make a minimum place for criticism, orthodoxy has insisted that what was inspired and hence error-free was the original text—the autograph, not the manuscripts on which all printed editions of the Bible are based.[4] But this is a useless distinction because no autograph has existed for centuries and it is vain to expect one to be found. Moreover, since in this view the distinctiveness of the Bible rests squarely on divine action, the authority of the Bible is separated from the historical activity of the church in creating the canon; that is, the canonizing process is reduced to a series of ecclesial acknowledgments. The intimate relation between church and canon, which historical criticism has made clear, is never allowed to appear fully. Inevitably, historical criticism came to be accepted only within limits determined by a theological a priori. Whoever preaches from such a stance toward the Bible will become a casuist, striving to relate an ahistorical, error-free, wholly self-consistent, miraculous text to the vicissitudes of historical existence today. It would be interesting to know to what extent such preaching, which one can only call an *ab*use of the Bible, has contributed to its *dis*use by those who can no longer share this perspective.

Although the role of biblical criticism in the emergence of this situation cannot be denied, it would be wrong to conclude that the solution is a crusade against biblical criticism, if for no other reason than the fact that one cannot restore the *status quo ante*. The task, rather, is to achieve a standpoint from which biblical criticism can be affirmed unhesitatingly while at the same time maintaining and clarifying the Bible's status as canon. Instead of repudiating biblical criticism in order to recover the authority of the Bible, it is necessary, and possible, to reconstitute the canonicity of the Bible on a basis that accords with what we have come to know about the Bible. That will be the task of chapter 3.

Finally, the most important factor in the present malaise of preaching is *the preacher's own ambivalence toward the Bible and toward biblical criticism.* Clearly, this is the nub of the matter because so long as this double ambivalence exists, those who preach will scarcely be motivated to develop their preaching in a deliberately biblical direction. This book, therefore, undertakes to deal with various aspects of the matter.

Since the preacher's ambivalence is the key factor in the emergence of the current malaise of biblical preaching, we shall reflect on it more extensively. It is, of course, even more difficult to make sound generalizations about preachers than about churches. Nonetheless, it will be useful to consider the matter from three standpoints: (a) the preacher whose ambivalence concerns, not the Bible, but biblical criticism; (b) the one who, somewhat like the churches noted above, finds that accepting biblical criticism has produced ambivalence about the Bible itself; (c) the preacher who is ambivalent about both the Bible and the critical method. The relation between these standpoints will be noted as we proceed.

Ambivalence about biblical criticism. Many, perhaps the vast majority, of the Protestant clergy have their roots in conservative piety where the Bible is revered as a holy book. For them, the encounter with biblical criticism was sometimes painful. If one concludes that Pentateuch was not written by Moses, the Fourth Gospel by John, or the Pastorals by Paul, and if one sees why Daniel was written four centuries later than it claims and that Jesus did not say everything attributed to him by the Gospels—how can one preach the Bible convincingly? Not a few concluded that not only their preaching ministry was threatened but their faith as well.

This situation has affected the teaching of the Bible in seminaries, especially since many of the teachers have had virtually the same religious backgrounds as these anxious students. Frequently, a considerable amount of time was devoted to defending criticism or its conclusions. Some teachers sought ways to "let them down gently," while others delighted in shock tactics. Either way, the basic strategy was the same—to impart a critical approach to Scripture (and the results of criticism) while at the same time reconstructing the faith and theology of the students. In more conservative contexts, the faculty have been on guard lest they appear to be "too critical"; in more liberal schools the conservative students were careful not to appear antediluvian in the presence of their peers and mentors, and so simply learned what was deemed necessary to pass the course but kept the appropriation of criticism to a minimum.

Such an experience of biblical study does not lay a good foundation for biblical preaching because the central issue has not been faced and worked through: What kind of Bible do we really have, and how does one preach from it convincingly and effectively? What is the authority of such a Bible for theology and ethics? Should a student from a conservative tradition seek answers to such questions, he or she might well find that professors of Bible are not necessarily adept in clarifying issues of systematic theology, that the professors of systematic theology, or ethics or homiletics, are either interested in other questions (having worked through such matters for themselves years ago), or may not be sufficiently conversant with current biblical criticism to engage the student at the appropriate points. Such a student often leaves seminary with an ingrained ambivalence: he or she continues to treasure the Bible and may also come to appreciate biblical criticism but does not know how far to take it.

As these young preachers proceed into the ministry, they will probably read those commentaries and books which perpetuate this ambivalence, or those whose attacks on "radical critics" (how often has this brand been put on Bultmann, for example?) reassure the reader that all is well so long as one stays with "conservative criticism." When it comes to teaching the Bible to the congregation, they may well shield the laity from biblical criticism, often on the grounds that "my people wouldn't know how to handle it." Actually, it is the preachers who do not know how to handle it. As a result, preaching from the Bible may gravitate toward passages that appear to offer no serious critical issues, or critical questions may simply be ignored in the process of sermon preparation. There are other possibilities, to be sure; but these suffice to suggest what is involved in this ambivalence toward criticism.

Ambivalence about the Bible. This ambivalence often has exactly the same origin as the previous one—conservative piety. Here, however, a full acceptance of biblical criticism produces an ambivalence toward the Bible itself. Whereas some theological students from a conservative background have found biblical criticism threatening, others have found it liberating. They have discovered that it helps them deal with questions that bothered them, and they feel freed from the burden of an external authority in the shape of a black book with gilt edges. The prophets, Jesus, and Paul are no longer oracles of timeless obligatory dogmas but humans grappling with issues that were intensely timely in their day.

It is not uncommon for this eager appropriation of biblical criticism, especially of its skepticism at certain historical points, to be part of a rejection of one's entire past, part of the emancipation from mother's religion. It is often accompanied by parallel revolts in theological stance, attitudes toward the institutional church, and against inherited mores of personal conduct. In such cases, the role of biblical criticism (indeed of historical thinking in the wide sense) is essentially negative (though the process may be positive) because it provides an umbrella under which one can rebel against childhood piety. Nor is it uncommon for preachers to arrest their maturation in rebellion instead of moving ahead to claim their legacy afresh, after having been distanced from it. Such a preacher could easily adapt the Pharisee's prayer, "Lord, I thank thee that I am no longer the pious conservative I once was. I know that some psalms were composed for the enthronement festival borrowed from Mesopotamia. I know that II Corinthians is a compilation of at least four letter fragments. I know that most of the Fourth Gospel does not report accurately Jesus' words. Above all, I am thankful that I have been liberated from my past by what I know."

Such preachers may develop a clear ambivalence about the Bible itself, stemming from the fact that they do not wish to reject its authority out of hand while at the same time being proud of the emancipation from biblical authoritarianism which has occurred through critical study. Thus they might speak fulsomely about "the biblical point of view" or of "the biblical understanding of X" (and quote safe passages only). Being liberals now, they will probably prefer abstractions like "the Judeo-Christian tradition" or "Jesus' principle of love" or the like. These can, of course, be linked to the Bible. However, this procedure is formally quite similar to that of the most accomplished proof-texter. Whereas the latter cites verses to guarantee dogmas, the former will cite passages that appear to cast an aura of biblical authority over principles, abstractions, and ideals connected only loosely with the Bible. Either way, the Bible is merely being raided, and its use is as unbiblical in the one instance as in the other.

If our emancipated friends teach the Bible to the congregation, they will probably try to liberate the pious from their conservative views as they too have been liberated. They will emphasize courses on "How we got our Bible" or explain and justify the Two-Source Theory of the Synoptic Gospels, and regard it as a major victory if they can get people to start speaking of Deutero-Isaiah. But these preachers may scarcely know how to help the congregation study the Bible as its Scripture, as its canon, inasmuch as it has lost much of its canonical status for them long ago; only the aura of authority remains. In the meantime, other books and journals have become the real canon of their ministry.

Ambivalence about both the Bible and biblical criticism. Both types of theological student and preacher we have considered carry a conservative, pious, devout legacy within themselves, acknowledged or not; for both it mattered what the professors of Bible did with the Scripture. Frequently, such ministers also carry within them a solid knowledge of its contents as well; many "came up through the ranks," having participated in church schools, youth groups, camps and conferences, and campus religious activities. In some denominations they have been lay preachers while in college, and some have been preaching since puberty. The one might have gotten a mild dose of criticism, the other a full one; the one might have been open to a minimum of criticism, which would allow him or her to be literate without having the whole religious structure threatened, whereas the other might have been eager for criticism to liberate him or her from traditional piety. Either way, for both it mattered what was being said about the Bible because each already had a traditional knowledge of it and relation to it.

The third type of ambivalence, however, emerges from a rather different soil. In recent years, there has been a growing number of theological students and young ministers who generally lack this "churchy" legacy, often totally. Some of these students are actually products of "liberal" churches, whose education and youth programs imparted only a smattering of Bible at best. Others have "secular" backgrounds, with virtually no experience of the church from the inside. Their interest in ministry was awakened in connection with college courses in religion, or in relation to various forms of "activism." Their motivation for ministry is often deep and their religious commitment as supple, though often unformed, as that of the more traditional student. But for them, the Bible is neither treasure nor baggage. They are simply strangers to it. They may leave seminary as ambivalent about the Bible as they arrived— knowing that it is somehow important and having learned some things about problems of interpreting it, but not having discovered that what is in the Bible is worth all that critical work to get at it.

Because a significant segment of the liberal Protestant clergy find themselves among this third group with respect to the Bible, and because there is so little communication between them and the first group, it is worthwhile to reflect further on the situation of this group with respect to the Bible and hence biblical preaching as well. Moreover, in interpreting this situation important aspects of the Bible in relation to preaching emerge that otherwise might elude consideration.

To begin with, we need to grasp the import of the fact that the primary context in which the emergent preachers in the third group develop a relation to the Bible is the classroom, not the church. In the classroom the Bible is an object to be analyzed, a complex phenomenon to be accounted for and explained historically. The entire battery of critical methods has been developed in order to carry out the various steps of this analytical, historical process. The person who does not bring a lifelong relationship with the Bible to the classroom experiences the historical-critical method quite differently than does the more traditional, church-nurtured student. As already noted, for the latter, criticism can be either a threat or a liberation, but for the former it can be primarily an obstacle to establishing a significant relation with the Bible at all before going out into the ministry. The reason is not obscure: critical analysis can modify the "authority" that the Bible already has, but criticism cannot generate a religiously significant relationship to it—nor should it be expected to.

When Walter Wink charged that biblical criticism is bankrupt,[5] he had in view just this situation—that criticism did not establish a life-nourishing relation to the Bible or to its real subject matter. The observation is correct enough, and equally off base because criticism is not designed to yield personal growth in the Christian faith. Such maturation may indeed occur, and often does; but when this happens, other factors are at work in the process.

Students with such "secular" backgrounds find it exceedingly difficult to do two things simultaneously in the classroom: master the critical method, which requires a certain distancing of oneself from the text; and establish an intimate religious relationship to the text which is necessary for biblical preaching. (The nature of this relationship will be the theme of the next chapter.)

Moreover, in a seminary the fledgling preacher who did not grow up with the Bible is expected to acquire simultaneously a basic knowledge of the content of the Bible and a working competence in biblical criticism, and to do so at a time when criticism is more sophisticated and complex than ever before. Not only is one expected to learn the difference between text, form, and redaction criticism (and in some settings, structuralism as well), but one needs to be literate enough about archaeological data, Dead Sea Scrolls, and Nag Hammadi gospels to be able to see the Bible in its cultural setting. For the novice, the dual task appears to be overwhelming and perhaps arbitrary as well. Furthermore, the student is expected to achieve this double competence within the framework of a curriculum that has generally minimized the importance of doing so, since required courses in Bible have been reduced to the absolute minimum in many schools. It would be interesting to learn how many persons graduated from theological seminaries during the past decade without ever having written an exegesis paper—to say nothing of having learned to work with the text in the original languages. Given the lack of background in the Bible on the one hand, and given the highly sophisticated and specialized nature of biblical scholarship today, on the other, it is understandable that many students would be much more attracted to courses in medical ethics, church and urban problems, religion and the arts, or theology of revolution. As a result a person can enter the ministry and begin preaching with a much better grasp of Peter Berger or Jürgen Moltmann than of Paul or Isaiah. The consequences for the ministry of preaching from the Bible are obvious.

Finally, a person who enters the ministry without having

been nurtured in the church or without a lifelong relation to the Bible has virtually no firsthand experience of the multiple roles that the Bible plays in the life of the church. Understandably, the church appears to be "stuck" with the Bible. The language of the hymns and liturgies appears strange and arbitrary because the biblical resonance is missing. The rich legacy of Christian worship and devotion remains obscure until this is overcome. In the presence of the materials in which previous Christians expressed themselves through the idiom of biblical language, this emerging pastor remains a bewildered and impoverished onlooker instead of a latter-day participant. The situation might be corrected in part if participation in worship were a significant part of the seminary experience, and if this worship itself were deliberately designed to socialize the community into the rich Christian heritage. But given the push toward experimentation in worship, to say nothing of attendance patterns, seminary chapel is scarcely the place to look for a corrective.

In light of these considerations, it is little wonder that the persons we have been considering find themselves as ambivalent about the Bible as about biblical criticism.

The amount of attention given to the third ambivalence does not mean that this group of ministers bears major responsibility for the malaise of biblical preaching. Nor should it be inferred that the seminaries are to blame for it all. There is enough blame to go around, to be sure; however, the aim here has been not to point accusatory fingers, but to understand the situation, and to show why one is justified in speaking of a malaise in biblical preaching. Yes, one can always think of exceptions—which, of course, simply establishes the main point, precisely because they are exceptions.

On the Malaise of Biblical Preaching
The High Price of the Malaise

Both the *mis*use of the Bible and its *dis*use have serious consequences for the health of Christianity. We shall note briefly three areas in which it is manifest that unless the present malaise is reversed, the price of drifting along will prove to be exceedingly high.

First of all, the most important thing at stake in the present state of biblical preaching is the vitality and authenticity of the gospel. One does not need to be particularly astute to see that, apart from various notable exceptions, main-line churches seem to be running out of steam. To be sure, factors other than the state of biblical preaching are involved. Nor does one need to be clairvoyant to regard with deep misgivings the fate of the gospel precisely among the churches that are thriving with a seemingly full head of steam. Doubtless Christianity can go to seed in many ways and for diverse reasons. In any case, centuries of experience show that apart from steady and significant engagement with the Bible, the church drops the ball—be it ever so "successful" in appearance. That is, the gospel is dissipated and distorted. Since the church lives by the gospel, failing to engage the Bible steadily and significantly brings with it a fundamental loss of the gospel.

The reason for this is no secret. It is the double fact that it is the Bible which identifies the fundamental lineaments of the gospel and that the church never possesses the gospel as a commodity but must discover repeatedly what "gospel" actually means. Apart from serious engagement with the Bible there is simply no way of testing whether what seems like good news in a given era is in fact the gospel.

It would be ridiculous to claim that the present trend would be reversed either when the fundamentalists accept biblical criticism or when the liberals preach "more Bible."

The Bible in the Pulpit

After all, criticism as such is neither the savior nor the lord of the church; furthermore, the Bible itself contains enough passages that can jeopardize the gospel if one does not know how to "discern the spirits" even within the canon. Nonetheless, for reasons that I hope to make clear as we proceed, recovering biblical preaching that accords with the kind of Scripture criticism has shown the Bible to be can go a long way toward alleviating the present pathology of the church. Unless this happens, there may be no viable future for Christianity in our time. What will thrive instead is a congery of religious entrepreneurs hawking their salvations on the one hand, and increasingly burdensome and otiose ecclesiastical organizations on the other.

Second, unless biblical preaching is recovered, the church as a whole will continue to suffer from amnesia. True, those strands of Christianity which have strong liturgical traditions have links to the past other than the Bible. But in other churches, the Bible is virtually the only link to historic Christianity.

The amnesia is real. Its most obvious symptom is the almost complete ignorance of the Bible in the church. This has been noted, lamented, and joked about so often that we need but mention it. Still, its consequences are devastating in the long run. If Christians are out of touch with their past in the Christian tradition, especially as it is canonized in Scripture, they lose their identity—precisely as do persons who are victimized by amnesia. Congregations with a loss of memory degenerate into societies for servicing their own religious dispositions, with a minimum of budgeting for "benevolences." They scarcely know who they are or what they are expected to be or to whom or what they are accountable. What Elizabeth Achtemeier described (see above, p. 19) is nothing other than amnesia of many contemporary liberal Protestant churches.

On the Malaise of Biblical Preaching

It is customary to blame the demise of biblical preaching on the fact that the congregations no longer "know their Bibles." This is, preachers justify bypassing biblical preaching by blaming the laity. It is true enough that biblical preaching cannot thrive in a vacuum, just as it is true that the sermon must not be confused with a lecture about the Bible. Nonetheless, the question remains: Whose responsibility is it to educate the laity in the Bible? Abandoning biblical preaching simply reinforces the pervasive ignorance so often decried. The fact remains, however, that for many people, the Sunday morning service is the main contact with the church. If the sermon, week after week, manifests a basic disregard for the Bible (apart from a decorative use of its language) in order to be "relevant," inevitably the hearers will conclude that the Bible and relevance have scarcely anything to do with each other.

Amnesia can also be found among those who emphasize the Bible in their sermons and among those who hear primarily expository preaching. This amnesia takes a quite different form because it is linked to the refusal to grant that the Bible is historically conditioned. In such a perspective the church lives by the illusion that it believes exactly what the biblical writers believed. There is no consciousness of time and contingency at either end of the arc; instead, one believes that there is direct access to the divinely given holy book inserted into history, and that our own histories do not put lenses between ourselves and the text. Thus Baptists readily assume that of course New Testament Christians were Baptists too; likewise Lutherans assume that the early church was essentially Lutheran, and Pentecostals know that it was pervasively charismatic. Teetotalers take it for granted that at Cana, Jesus turned water into unfermented grape juice, just as some Anglo-Catholics know full well that the early Christians were as concerned about proper ordination as they are.

One of the functions of historical criticism is to overcome both kinds of amnesia by making us intensely conscious of the historicity of Christian faith all along the line. Historical criticism confronts both that form of amnesia which is virtually cut off from the historic rootage of the faith in order to celebrate the present, and that form which cuts off the historicity of the biblical root in order to relate itself unhistorically to an unhistorical Bible. Unless both forms of amnesia are overcome, it is difficult to see how Christianity can breed true to itself.

Third, the present malaise of biblical preaching exacts a high price from the vocational identity of the preacher. To be sure, disciplined biblical preaching is an art based on exacting work. The meaning of the Bible is seldom self-evident and rarely exhausted; one must exegete the text again and again. Moreover, one should live with the text, brood on its assumptions and import, ponder the similarity between the experiences of its first readers and those of today. If effective biblical preaching costs so much effort, how then can one say that neglect of biblical preaching exacts a high price in the long run? Would it not be more fair to say that neglecting biblical preaching is less costly than undertaking it? Not at all.

For one thing, the preacher who neglects biblical preaching falls prey to incipient clericalism and gnosticism with regard to the Bible; curiously, the one who preaches the Bible unbiblically is vulnerable at the same point. At first glance, nothing would seem more alien to both the left and the right than clericalism, because neither is known for its high regard for ordination or a sacramental view of the ministry. Rather, both have been vulnerable to entrepreneurs with sufficient charisma to generate their own churches and clienteles. But that is precisely the phenomenon that gives the secret away: in both cases, whether on the left or on the right, the churches know only that about the Bible which the preacher wants them to know. Neither entrusts the Bible to the church by the way it is dealt with in the pulpit. Thus the preacher becomes a kind of shaman who alone knows how to handle the dangerous thing properly. (It is hard to know who would be more nervous—a fundamentalist preacher who discovered that one of his key lay persons was secretly studying Fosdick's *Modern Use of the Bible,* or a liberal preacher who learned that the chairperson of the social action committee was taking a correspondence course in Bible prophecy from a radio preacher.)

This clericalism is intimately linked with a form of gnosticism, because in either case the preacher has access to privileged information. In hyper-conservative churches, only the preacher knows how to decipher all the allegorical symbolism of Israel's tabernacle in the wilderness as a prefiguration of Christ's atonement. In liberal churches, where information about the Bible is freely imparted, scarcely anyone but the preacher will know what to make of the mass of historical information and the critical theories about the Pentateuch. The former, of course, is eager to impart a saving gnosis, whereas the latter may be eager to develop a circle of cognoscenti. The Bible is just as esoteric and mysterious when it must be decoded by the preacher who finds all sorts of secret symbols in it as it is when it becomes such a mass of complex theories about strata, genres, influences, and the like that people think it impossible for them to get into it with profit. In neither case is the church enabled to come to terms with its own scripture, unless the preacher tells them what it all means. In such a case, the minister of the Word has become the guardian of the gnosis. That, in my judgment, is too high a price to pay for neglecting the regular discipline of preaching the Bible biblically, of sharing with the congregation the agony and the joy of discovering its power.

Perhaps the highest price will be exacted from the minister as a person. What nurtures his or her own life, expands the horizons, and puts steel into the spine when that is called for? When churches call preachers or bishops appoint them, ascertaining some sort of answer to that question might be just as important, and far more revealing, as learning the statistics from the previous parish. In any case, churches, being part of the institutional life of society, are sufficiently jungle-like that preachers need survival kits if they are not to become mere functionaries or pitchmen. There is, to be sure, a wealth of literature, art, music, and drama that has the capacity to expand and renew the soul, and each person probably finds his or her own array of such materials to turn to. Still, the preacher who neglects the Bible as the bread of his or her own life may find that regardless of how many attractive delicacies one serves each Sunday, one may be suffering from malnutrition. On the other hand, the one who preaches the Bible biblically usually finds himself confronted by more bread "than one can say grace over."

This chapter has sought to identify certain elements in the situation in which this book is written and to which it is addressed. Neither in tracing the factors that have generated the present malaise of biblical preaching, nor in noting briefly some of the consequences, has it been implied that the demise of biblical preaching is the only malaise affecting the health of the church today. Nor do I want to suggest that the development of biblical preaching would be a miracle drug that, if taken in proper dosage, would swiftly restore vitality and power to the church. No single step can be expected to carry the whole load. It has been suggested, however, that this would be a significant step toward the renewal of the church, and a necessary one as well.

In the chapters that follow, we shall address certain aspects of the promise of biblical preaching. Instead of beginning with a definition of biblical preaching, however, we shall first focus on the role of the preacher and his or her relation to the Bible. Then, in chapter 3, we shall explore the nature of the Scripture. That will provide the basis for answering the root question, What makes preaching biblical (chapter 4)?

Chapter Two

The Liberation of Lazarus

Far too frequently, today's preacher stands in the pulpit like a modern Lazarus: "His hands and feet [were] bound with bandages, and his face wrapped with a cloth." He is immobilized and shows no face to the public. As John tells it, Jesus said, "Unbind him, and let him go." Can that happen to Lazarus in the pulpit?

If we were to choose a New Testament figure to symbolize who we think we are as we stand in the pulpit, we would certainly not pick Lazarus. We might see ourselves as Paul on Mars Hill, subtly leading the Athenian intelligentsia to the point where the gospel's claim confronts them; or Paul before Agrippa, boldly defending his calling and bearing witness to the gospel before civil authorities. Others would like to see themselves as Apollos, "eloquent and well-versed in the Scriptures." Some might even dare to identify with Philip, who was not ashamed to be seen riding with an Ethiopian eunuch. But this Lazarus, all wrapped up?

But I suspect that there is more of Lazarus in most of us than there is of Paul, Apollos, or Philip. More important, I suspect that what we need most of all is liberation from those wrappings which inhibit us, which keep us from being alive, germane, and articulate in the pulpit. Lazarus is a symbol of the plight of the preacher and of preaching today when the spoken word is inhibited in its power and inarticulate in its content. The question is whether Lazarus will be unwrapped so that preaching, and specifically biblical preaching, will become vital again.

The Liberation of Lazarus

To be sure, there *is* vital preaching being done today, even if "princes of the pulpit" are difficult to name, and even if there is little consensus about the criteria of "good preaching." Does one gauge preaching by its style and rhetorical power? Is not the criterion of good preaching a subjective one, and therefore a matter of taste, like "good music"? And do not the criteria of vital preaching vary from one setting to the next, so that what is considered good preaching in a largely white, suburban Protestant church differs considerably from what would be regarded as good preaching in a black Baptist church? Are the standards for preaching in evangelical churches the same as in liberal ones or in Catholic parishes? Even when due allowance has been made for such considerations, however, one still detects widespread dismay over the state of preaching. Preachers themselves often admit that this element of their vocation is in general disarray, and many congregations would agree even if they are unclear about what they would regard as good preaching. Wittingly or otherwise, many preachers have become accomplices in the undoing of their craft; they have acquiesced in the making of Lazarus.

It would be grotesque to allegorize the figure of Lazarus in relation to today's preacher, for then we would exhibit precisely an improper way to use the Bible, and would probably bypass much of what is important in the situation as well. Instead, we shall use the image of Lazarus as a metaphor for the preacher whose preaching is inhibited more by internal factors than by external constraints (an allegorical use of Lazarus would see him as the victim of extraneous limitations, the "bandages"). This chapter intends to show why the preacher's own relation to the Bible is the key to a renewal of biblical preaching, and thereby of preaching generally. Before dealing with this topic directly, however, it will be useful to reflect a bit on what may presently be standing in the way of Lazarus's freedom to preach biblically.

Lazarus Bound

To begin with, many preachers today have lost confidence in the importance of preaching. Preachers are justified in feeling themselves, and this aspect of their vocation, to be victimized by cultural changes that they cannot control or even moderate. To be concrete, the fundamental change in the rhythm of life has brought about a decline in the importance of Sunday as the day of rest and church attendance. Between staggered work schedules, on the one hand, and more long weekends devoted to recreation, on the other, regular church attendance has suffered markedly, especially in urban and suburban areas. Moreover, TV has made it ever more difficult for people to attend carefully to merely verbal communication, except perhaps for sports on radio. Many people find it difficult to follow a panel discussion unless there is sharp controversy. Unless the speaker has "charisma," his or her televised speech is not likely to hold a viewing audience for long. The spot commercial and the interview fare somewhat better, especially if they are humorous. TV, after all, is programmed mainly for entertainment. This loss of attentiveness to verbal communication, to oral discourse, has eroded the place of the sermon. The black church is an exception, for there it is often customary for the congregation to participate in the preaching with its "amens" and "right ons"; to some extent, the same must be conceded to white "pentecostal" churches as well. It is the staid, sophisticated, main-line white Protestant churches that have been affected most. The preacher knows this quite well, and sometimes painfully; it has eroded the sense that preaching is important. Perhaps he or she has conceded too much too soon. Be that as it may, where there is no confidence in the importance of the art, the preacher begins to function like Lazarus.

In the second place, many preachers have been deeply affected by a general revolt against authority and against persons in positions of authority. Again, the exceptions reinforce this generalization when we bear in mind that in many black churches, and in conservative white ones as well, the preacher is still an authority figure who is expected to deliver a "thus saith the Lord" with no hedging. But for significant segments of Protestantism, the idea of a person behind a high (or low) pulpit, telling people what the truth is and what they are to believe and strive for, is far too authoritarian to be acceptable. Have we not been urged repeatedly to do our own thing, to discern for ourselves what is true for us and to discover it by discussion? If something is worth communicating, don't spoil it by preaching it! Let it emerge in the give-and-take of the group; celebrate it by music, dance, or drama. In preaching, people are as passive as chickens on a roost—and perhaps just as awake. For whatever reason, the authority of the preacher has become problematic.

In the third place, our Lazarus may also be bound by a more subtle perception, namely, the sense of incongruity between lived experience and orderly presentation of the sermon.[1] We shall not cheapen this point by mocking the sermon with three points framed by introduction and conclusion and sprinkled with appropriate illustrations for each sub-point. What is in view here is just as true of a two-part or four-point sermon. The point is that good preaching, like good public speaking in general, is characterized by clarity and orderly presentation, and frequently by simplicity as well. Indeed, one often wishes for more clarity and order in place of the rambling remarks that can suggest to the hearer that the preacher is still hoping that the sermon will jell as he or she speaks. In any case, both the congregation and the preacher sensitized by pastoral experience have an intuitive sense that life lacks the very things that the sermon needs: order, coherence, and clarity. The clearly wrought sermon seems to imply that truth is rational, consistent, and reducible to a limited number of points. This, however, seems to confer an aura of unreality to the sermon. The clearer and simpler the sermon, the more artificial it may seem. This is because, instinctively, many persons believe that truth is glimpsed momentarily and in fragments, that it lacks symmetry, that it is awkward and angular as it breaks through to us; they sense that frustrations and ambiguities dog our choices, and tentativeness marks our commitments.

True, it is common stragegy for preachers to take note of life's incoherences and absurdities only to "answer" them clearly, to resolve complex moral and religious issues simply. After all, what more can one do in twenty minutes? Besides, sermons, like many movies, are expected to have a happy ending, at least a positive and inspiring one. The sort of ending that the movie *Easy Rider* has appears to be unthinkable in a sermon. The more one is impressed by the inchoate character of life and by the raw edges of life's irrationality, the less confidence will the preacher (and the congregation) have in the very form of the clearly crafted sermon. It may strike one as a brief stroll through never-never land. Here too the Bible can be used unbiblically, especially when its heroes are portrayed as ever stalwart believers whose high achievements and allegedly simple answers are to be the norm for the present-day church.

Fourth, we need to explore further the minister's situation with respect to the Bible and biblical criticism which we noted in the previous chapter. Two aspects of this merit reflection here: (a) the impact on the preacher's own certitude and self-image as an interpreter of the Bible and the Christian faith; (b) the preacher's own relation to the eroded certitude of which he or she may be acutely conscious.

The loss of certitude that is sometimes linked with exposure to biblical criticism is part of a much larger pattern, as already noted. What was once taken for granted or affirmed unhesitatingly—not only the Bible but the basic tenets of the Christian faith—is seldom the same for the person who has stepped back two paces to look at the matter critically and in light of its historical character. Whatever element of the belief structure of the Christian faith one turns to—such as immortality/resurrection, incarnation, or sacraments—historical thinking has shown how each of them evolved across many decades and was subject to various influences in the process. Thus, the idea of immortality conferred by resurrection appears first in the latest parts of the Old Testament, incarnation is not taught by the Synoptics, and sacramental theology owes a great deal more to Hellenistic cults than to the Old Testament heritage. Perceptions such as these prompted the famous radical nineteenth-century critic, D. F. Strauss, to formulate it this way: "The criticism of dogma is its history." Recently, Hans Frei has argued astutely that ever since the eighteenth century, the Bible, and the elements of the Christian faith as well, are less and less the lens through which we perceive reality and have become more and more problematic "objects" of analysis and interpretation. The biblical story no longer interprets us and our world; now we find it necessary to interpret the biblical story.[2]

It would be rash to claim that an analysis of a representative cross section of the clergy would reveal conscious grappling with such issues. Indeed, part of the difficulty, one suspects, is that the issues are sensed but neither defined nor discussed openly; in such cases, they readily gnaw silently, like cancer. The preacher who perceives the Bible, or the inherited belief structure of Christian theology, primarily as a set of problems readily loses inner confidence even though one may be quite certain about a number of individual beliefs. The more aware one becomes of the ways in which the Christian faith is shaped by the texture of its own history and of our culture—history that can be traced through four millennia and across several cultures and language systems—the less obvious it is just what it all amounts to today.

It will repay us to linger a bit longer here. No one can read the Bible in relation to its own times without becoming aware of certain fundamental strangeness (similarities and parallels also exist,as we shall see). It is sufficient to mention the most obvious in order to be concrete: a pre-Copernican view of the universe in which the earth is the center and which has subterranean quarters for the dead, whereas God and the angels live "upstairs" beyond the heavenly bodies; unexplained assumptions about the power of animal blood, when properly used, to remove human sin; miracle stories of all sorts, ranging from wondrous healing of fever to a floating ax head; a God who hates as well as loves, seeks vengeance as well as reconciliation; an assortment of eschatological views which are only superficially similar to both certain aspects of current nihilism and optimism about the future. There is much else in the Bible to be sure, but these materials are there too and sometimes provide the framework for the whole.

Modern Christian theology has grappled with these matters ever since the eighteenth century, for it has seen that a fundamental task is finding ways to reinterpret this Bible and the theological tradition as a whole. Nor is it accidental that the landmarks of Christian theology have been achieved by theologians deeply concerned for preaching.

The Liberation of Lazarus

We recall that Schleiermacher, commonly regarded as the fountainhead of modern Protestant theology, wrote his systematic theology while he preached Sunday after Sunday in Berlin. A century later, his critic, Karl Barth, became a theologian because of the demands placed on his conscience and mind by the responsibility of preaching in a Swiss village. Bultmann's famous demythologizing proposal reflects his deep commitment to the task of preaching the gospel so that it could get through to moderns as gospel, not as fairy tales or miracle stories. Each in his own way knew that articulate preaching of the gospel always occurs in intimate relation to theological clarity and consistency, and that a major task of theology is to provide a coherent conceptual framework within which the Bible can be interpreted and the gospel proclaimed.

Today's preacher, however, lacks a prevailing theological framework because ours is a time of theological chaos. The heyday of "neo-orthodoxy," whether in its Barthian or Niebuhrian form, is past—perhaps prematurely and probably to our loss in important respects. Gone too is the "history of salvation" theology, commonly associated with the "biblical theology movement," whose demise has been interpreted ably by Brevard Childs.[3] The bloom is off existentialist theology associated with Bultmann; and even the much-heralded "post-Bultmannian" theology, attributed to Ernst Fuchs and Gerhard Ebeling, also appears passé. Despite considerable ballyhoo, neither Pannenberg's theology nor Cone's, nor "process theology," led by Cobb and his followers, has come to prevail. Instead, in an era of faddism, one theological proposal after another is "queen for a day." Each year we have bought a new paperback entitled *New Theology No. ___*. The busy preacher scarcely begins to explore the possibilities of a new theology when he learns that it has already become an

Edsel. Many continuing education programs, including the D.Min. degrees, are so largely oriented toward the development of ministerial praxis that they have scarcely addressed the hermeneutical/theological task at all—if indeed they even know it exists. In short, we live amid the disintegration of the Christian tradition. We need not wear sackcloth and ashes for this state of affairs, because we are probably experiencing the prelude to a renewal and renovation whose shape is not yet visible.

In any case, when the sensitive preacher sees the theological framework in shambles, he or she may well begin to wonder what one is to preach. Nor is it surprising that many a preacher's theology appears to be a jerry-built hodgepodge, or that sermons seem not to reflect a sustained and coherent engagement with root problems of interpretation. Probably many ministers are keenly aware of these things, since they must stand in the pulpit week after week where they are expected to have something significant and positive to say on the widest range of topics. But awareness of the difficulty is not yet professional competence in addressing the issues. And doubtless there are others who have only a vague feeling that all is not well, while yet others—especially the younger ones—know it all too painfully as they struggle to find themselves.

The preacher, of course, lives in the same culture as everyone else, and the same mentality that shapes the horizons of people in and out of the church shapes those of the preacher as well. Indeed the preacher who has a good college education in the humanities at the base of his or her theological degree is keenly aware of the chasm between "modernity" and the assumptions and assertions of the classical Christian tradition. Precisely because good education, in contrast to mere training, is critical by definition, the educated preacher has experienced a distancing from the claims of the religious faith he or she inherited. An irreversible relativizing has occurred wherever one has been made aware of the contingency and particularity of one's deeply held values and beliefs. This is no less true of religious beliefs than of social attitudes or political points of view. It is probably impossible to identify any specific belief, assumption, or value transmitted by the Christian tradition that has remained immune from some aspects of this process. The fuss generated a decade ago over the "death of God" revealed both the depth of the erosion and the anxiety generated by it. Moreover, it forced into the open what was there for a long time—that faith is a matter of personal commitment and conviction, and that one can no longer ride a cultural tide into the Christian faith.

Because the preacher is not insulated from this phenomenon and may well be especially sensitized to it, he or she must face up to his or her own relation to the inherited Christian faith. The preacher knows that the central task is to affirm the faith and to preach the gospel as persuasively as possible, not to display one's own doubts. But still, what is to be done with those doubts, those dry spells in one's inner life, the uncertainties about the meaning and validity of the whole tradition? One knows, of course, that life and faith are a matter of pilgrimage toward understanding and faithful discipleship, and that at no point is one a finished product. Yet, one must preach now, Sunday by Sunday. Some are expected to be evangelistic. I shall never forget the seminary student whom I asked at the beginning of his second year, "What did you do this summer?" This man, only at the initial stages of rebuilding his grasp of the Christian faith, gave a reply that I continue to regard as tragic: "I held five revivals." Evidently he was obligated to put into storage the amorphous character of his own faith so he could be properly evangelistic.

The preacher knows that many of the people in the pew wrestle with the same doubts and uncertainties as he or she does. It is tragic that often this does not draw pastor and people closer together because whatever doubts the people may have, they often want their preacher to believe it all, and to do so undeviatingly. They expect the preacher to be the super-Christian, and perhaps do their believing for them so that some of his or her faith will rub off on them. In any case, they go to church not to have their doubts and uncertainties confirmed by the preacher but to have them addressed and dealt with. It is no wonder that the preacher soon masters the art of role playing; it is a matter of survival.

The effect on one's preaching, however, can be devastating. One can, of course, stay away from themes and passages that create the most difficulties in order to preach what one can affirm. But how readily this produces a rather narrow range of preaching, especially if one does not use a lectionary. The result is all too familiar: week after week, one of three or four hobby horses is given a twenty-minute ride. Moreover, such a pattern inhibits the very growth that is needed, especially because one can always be "too busy" to give sustained attention to the issues. For such a minister, preaching can easily become a chore, and the preacher can become his or her own version of Lazarus.

This brief reflection on certain aspects of the Lazarus situation has not been undertaken to excoriate preachers! When all the criticisms and analyses are in, one must still admire the spritiual and moral stamina, and the attempts at faithfulness, that mark the profession as a whole. The preacher's task has grown ever more difficult. Nonetheless, there is too much of Lazarus in us to be ignored. The question is, Can Lazarus be freed? Can biblical preaching, and the discipline that underlies it, liberate Lazarus?

The Liberation of Lazarus

Lazarus Freed and Articulate

Lazarus will be unbound and preaching will be liberated when the preacher has something compelling to say, a subject matter that grasps the preacher so that he or she becomes a witness to it. The message makes the medium. So long as the message does not grasp the messenger, the person in the pulpit is a Lazarus, an immobile mumbler of other people's ideas.

The intimate relationship between the preacher and the message is a matter of some subtlety. Virtually everything one must say about this motif produces a counterpoint, a warning against abuse. Samples are abundant.

One must have a message that is truly one's own,	*but*	what is worse than a preacher whose message is really an idiosyncrasy?
A preacher can convince others only of what he or she is convinced of,	*but*	does the persuasive capacity of the good news rise and fall with the ebb and flow of the preacher's own convictions? Must he or she be the superbeliever before the gospel has power?
A preacher's message and his or her life and morals, and those of the preacher's family, must cohere, because the adage, "Physician, heal thyself!" is an immutable law;	*but*	does the credibility of the gospel really ride on the manifest moral perfection of the preacher and his or her family?

49

These examples really pose different aspects of one fundamental question: Is everybody justified by faith except the preacher? Is the preacher alone justified by works? It is precisely pressure to answer this affirmatively that has been a major factor in putting the wraps on Lazarus, for it imposes a burden on the preacher that no one can bear indefinitely. Where the preacher survives by cultivating a clear disjunction between the private self and the public self in the pulpit, there emerges the worst side of professionalism: like Lazarus, one shows no authentic face at all.

Now we can reformulate our theme as a question: What is this message which is so compelling that it grasps the preacher in such a way that his or her words and life give the witness of a free, authentic person? In speaking of justification faith, we have stated it—the gospel as interpreted by Paul. Concretely, appropriating the way Paul applies the gospel to himself liberates the preacher. Whoever is grasped by the Pauline gospel will preach credibly and authentically because it makes one a free person. This is an audacious claim. Paul, however, can liberate us only if we understand him, and to do so we shall go to Corinth. Despite the miles and the millennia between us, we shall be quite at home.

Paul's relationship with the church at Corinth was turbulent, and it degenerated to the point that eventually he felt compelled to write in irony and sarcasm. After Paul had left the city, other wandering apostles appeared in Corinth who undermined his work. They found the church receptive because the Corinthians had been grading their leaders according to demonstrable credentials. Paul had already dealt with this in I Corinthians 1–4, but he was not able to stem the tide. The apostles who arrived on the scene later were able to discredit Paul while at the same time enhancing their own status in the church. The Corinthians reached the point where they said that Paul writes a good letter but he himself is not very impressive (II Cor. 10:10). In contrast, these others really come on strong. They are impressive and eloquent; everyone can see how spiritual they are. Their preaching sparkles with stories of marvelous things they have done in the name of the Lord. No wonder Paul nicknames them "super-apostles" (II Cor. 11:5).

Modern parallels to the super-apostles are not hard to find. Nowadays too they come on strong. They gain credence and influence by proclaiming their mighty works, often healings or dramatic conversions of super-sinners that occurred through their preaching. They seem to travel in a gospel road show that features the famous converts.

Why does Paul insist that he will continue to undermine these super-apostles (II Cor. 11:12)? Let us not simply accuse him of professional jealousy. Rather, Paul sees that such attempts to *ac*credit the gospel actually *dis*credit it because they jeopardize the meaning of the cross. In order to make that clear, Paul finally agrees to play their game, and so begins to boast of his accreditation: five times he got thirty-nine lashes from Jews; three times the Romans put the rod to him; three times he endured shipwreck, once being adrift at sea for twenty-four hours, etc. (II Cor. 11:24-29). What Paul boasts of is not his apostolic achivements but his apostolic vulnerability; not his physical endurance ("Look what Jesus helped me do!") but his physical weakness. When he turns to experiences of the Spirit (much prized at Corinth), to his being caught up in ecstasy so that he sees Paradise itself, he immediately writes of his thorn in the flesh, and of the threefold prayer that was *not* answered on his terms. What is the point of this curriculum vitae of weakness? Paul himself says it: "I will all the more gladly boast of my weakness that the power of Christ may rest upon me" (II Cor. 12:9). Some months later, after the difficulty with Corinth had been worked out, he comes back to the same theme and explains it again: "We have this treasure in earthen vessels, to show that the transcendent power belongs to God and not to us" (II Cor. 4:7).

Let me restate Paul's point. Wherever the preacher displays his or her manifest spirituality, or great works of any sort, there the gospel is being jeopardized because the beholder is being asked to draw a one-to-one correlation between the power of the preacher and the power of the gospel. In such situations, the gospel is deemed weak when the preacher appears weak, effective when he or she is powerful. And it is precisely this correlation that jeopardizes the meaning of the cross, the center of the gospel, for according to Paul the cross means that "God chose what is low and despised in the world, . . . so that no human being might boast in the presence of God" (I Cor. 1:28-29). The critical meaning of the gospel of the cross/resurrection is that divine power cannot be inferred directly from human power.

Is there then no attesting evidence for the gospel? If there is, what kind of manifest evidence does not jeopardize the gospel itself? It is that strange dialectic of power through weakness, strength through vulnerability; it embodies discontinuity from the criteria of the day. Paul mentioned some of its manifestations: "When reviled, we bless; when persecuted, we endure; when slandered, we try to conciliate" (I Cor. 4:12-13). That "the kingdom of God does not consist in talk but in power" (I Cor. 4:20) becomes manifest where that dialectic, that disparity, occurs. If such a dialectic is absent, Paul implies, it will be equally manifest that the Kingdom has been turned into talk without power, irrespective of how many impressive deeds occur in its name. Where Paul is not heeded, the gospel and the preacher are soon justified by works, not by faith. Where

Paul is ignored, the preacher and the message inevitably rely on approval based on the standards of our market-oriented culture. In short, Paul has seen that one cannot justify the preacher and his or her message by the norms of the culture without surrendering the meaning of the cross.

In other words, the need of the preacher to be grasped by the message is not a pious thought but a dangerous demand. Whenever the preacher is not grasped by the word of the cross, one becomes what Paul calls a peddler, one who has the message at one's disposal as a commodity to be marketed as effectively as one can manage. As in Corinth, such a preacher ends up offering "another Jesus" (II Cor. 11:4), be one ever so orthodox otherwise. Paul discerned that if the message does not make the medium, the preacher, then in fact the medium becomes the message. That is, we preach the gospel in such a way that in the final analysis we proclaim ourselves.

What, then, is the liberating alternative? How is the preacher grasped by the gospel so that, as its medium, one is not the message but the witness to it? How is the preacher intimately involved with this message without interposing oneself between it and the hearers? With these questions, we are at the heart of the matter, where the liberation of Lazarus can occur. That this occurs in conjunction with biblical preaching and the discipline of preparation for it, is the burden of this chapter. (Whether, and to what extent, the same sort of liberation might occur by intensified attention to other kinds of preaching is a matter for someone else to worry about.)

From Priestly Listener to Prophetic Witness

The thesis being proposed can be stated tersely: *The preacher is a prophet who bears witness to what he or she has heard in his or her priestly role.* There are four elements in this thesis that call for comment.

First, biblical preaching flows from hearing. To preach biblically, one must first "hear" the text.

What comes into view here is the important, and subtle, distinction between preaching from a text that has been "heard" and merely reporting what it says or arguing on its behalf. A sermon does not become proportionately more biblical by the number of times the preacher can announce, "The Bible says. . . ." What makes a sermon biblical will be discussed further in the following chapters. Here we simply distinguish repeating the Bible's words from proclaiming what has been heard in those words. Making this distinction need not create a dichotomy between them because the Bible is a very diverse book. Its diverse literary forms—poetry, various kinds of narrative, laws, theological formulations, visions, for instance—evoke different responses. In some instances it is virtually impossible to preach a text without repeating the determinative terminology or its synonyms. In general, one may say that the more explicitly theological the text is, the more essential it is to remain within the range of the semantic equivalents. One can hardly preach passages that deal with creation or faith, for example, without using these words, including modern paraphrases of them. On the other hand, a sermon on the Ascension runs the risk of being unbiblical altogether if it simply repeats, and asserts vigorously, that Christ was raised up into heaven by the cloud. Moreover, the degree to which the explicit content of the text will be repeated also varies according to the intent of the sermon on a given occasion. Given the diversity of the Bible and of sermon situations, there is simply no way to prescribe in advance how much of the text's explicit content and vocabulary must be repeated in the sermon for it to be genuinely biblical. In any case, a biblical sermon is not a book report. It is a proclamation of what has been heard in and through the text.

In order to "hear" a text, one must cultivate the art of listening to it, with it, and through it. In other words, one must develop the skill and art of exegesis. Because it is not self-evident what exegesis is and what it entails, it is necessary to indicate briefly how the term is used here.

Scholars are sometimes divided over whether the task of exegesis is restricted to ascertaining "what it meant" or whether it includes saying "what it means." Two things can be said on behalf of the position that the scholar-exegete should restrict himself to describing "what it meant" to the author and his original readers irrespective of what present-day theologians, preachers, mystics, or artists may wish to make of it (or not make of it). One, concern for present meaning can easily lead the exegete to confuse the author's meaning with what the exegete wishes the text to mean. Two, many scholars have become experts in rather narrow fields of inquiry; even if they have a deep personal interest in the contemporary significance of the text, they may not regard themselves as sufficiently competent to articulate adequately that significance and so are content to place the results of their work at the disposal of those who are.

The pervasiveness of this pattern is manifest in several ways. For example, it characterizes the way Bible is taught in seminaries, partly because a faculty by definition embraces a range of specialties, each of which tends to respect the domain of the others. The biblical scholar tends to leave present-day theological meaning to colleagues in systematic theology, the current moral import to those in ethics or homiletics, and so on. Another place where this pattern shows up is in publications: *The Interpreter's Bible*, and the recent *Proclamation Series* published by Fortress Press, embody the division of labor by actually drawing a line between the Exegesis part and the Exposition part.

The consequences of this pattern are also apparent. Seminarians and preachers are often left with the impression that exegesis is an exercise in antiquity, and that commentaries are books in which one "looks up" a passage when certain obscurities are found. Since scholarly commentaries usually concentrate on annotations on details of the text and its historical or literary background, the preacher soon thinks that one gains little from them for sermon preparation; they offer few handles for making a connection between what it meant then and what it might mean today. One reason Bultmann was such a giant in the field was that he was able to combine first-rate historical critical analysis with a viable statement of what the text says now. Another unfortunate consequence is that the reader of commentaries gains the impression that once problematic details of language and matters of background are explained historically, the subject matter of the text is more or less self-explanatory. Few commentaries induce one to think through the subject matter with the biblical writer, or to wrestle with it. Because Karl Barth saw this problem clearly, his preface to the second edition of his commentary on Romans remains a landmark in the history of exegesis, for here he insisted that the exegete must go beyond the historical critical analysis and engage the content of Paul's argument in order to re-say it now.

Today there is growing interest in what is broadly called "structuralism"—an approach to texts that frequently disregards almost totally the historical question of "what it meant" originally and concentrates on what it "means"—an understanding of "meaning" that is essentially timeless because it is grounded in the structure of the human mind as it comes to particular expression in a given text. There are signs that structuralist exegesis might become a sectarian movement; nonetheless, it can be a wholesome counter-balance to excessive preoccupation with what lies behind the text or the intent of the writer. Because it focuses our attention on the text as it now exists, structuralism can enrich historical-critical exegesis, but it is doubtful whether it can, or should, displace it.[4]

Be that as it may, in this book it is primarily historical critical exegesis that is in view, partly because that is still the most widely understood meaning of the term "exegesis," partly because some preachers perceive historical criticism as the culprit in their frustration with biblical preaching, and partly because this mode of exegesis provides the clues to preaching the Bible in a biblical way.

This is not the place to spell out the steps in the exegetical process; with a colleague in Old Testament, I have sketched that elsewhere.[5] What does need to be done here is to state succinctly what exegesis is after and what it involves—that is, the sense in which the exegete is a listener.

The attentive listener is not passive, as any music lover, seasoned counselor, wise judge, or perceptive parent knows. Thanks to the ubiquitous tape recorder, we can learn to listen by playing and replaying a tape until "we really hear it." The activity of the exegete of a text is comparable to that of the listener who plays and replays a tape until he or she understands what is on it.

It may help us if we compare listening to a tape of a counseling session and listening to (exegeting) a biblical text. In both cases, the perceptive listening becomes an art as well as a skill only when certain principles are mastered so that they become second nature. One does not begin by listening on this level; one begins by learning what to listen for, what the important clues to meaning are, and by acquiring a conceptual framework within which what is heard becomes significant. Likewise, in both cases, the listener must acquire the ability to learn from the text or tape, and not assume prematurely that one understands what is going on. Furthermore, listeners to a tape and to a biblical text both discover that one seldom grasps the entire meaning; indeed the meaning of the text or tape seems to deepen as one's own perception develops. "Meaning," after all, is not just there like a vein of coal to be discovered and mined once and for all. Moreover, because the tape and the text are human documents that embody and articulate many layers of experience, the most important thing that both listeners must learn is to take absolutely nothing for granted. Precisely because the preacher acquires a growing familiarity with the Bible (one may hope!), and probably preaches from the same text repeatedly, he or she needs to guard against presuming to understand it. Developing this opening for the possibility of discovery and surprise is the most important dimension of learning to listen, because without it one merely hears confirmations.

Exegesis is nothing less than the art of asking fruitful questions of the text, and of doing so in an orderly way. This understanding of the matter is simply the obverse of ceasing to take the text for granted. Each of the specialized and sometimes rather sophisticated methods or procedures of biblical criticism has been developed in order to facilitate this process of asking and answering particular questions as best one can. The careful exegete has a plan, a series of questions designed and ordered in such a way as to account for the text as an historical event, to faciliate understanding what it meant when it came into existence. (The complex character of the phrase "when it came into existence" will become evident in the next chapter.)

Thus far the exegete is in effect *listening in on* the conversation between the biblical writer and his original readers; one is not yet *listening to it*. One begins to listen to the text when one is drawn into the discussion, when one must deal with the subject matter, engage its theme and in effect begin conversing with the text and its author. Not until this begins to occur does one really exegete—bring out the meaning. The essential rationale for undertaking the historical critical inquiry, and for doing so before one engages the text's subject matter, is this: to ascertain as precisely as possible what Isaiah or Paul himself was saying in the first place. If one is going to converse with Paul about faith, for instance, one must try first to discern what it was that Paul had to say on the subject and why he said it the way he did. Otherwise, one might not engage Paul at all but only what one assumes he was saying. Historical critical analysis is far from foolproof, and yields no permanently accurate results, as the history of criticism shows. Nonetheless, it is the only method we have by which to distinguish what Paul meant from what we assume he meant or wish he had meant. In short, the aim of historical critical exegesis is to hear the original meaning as clearly as possible in order to be able to respond, in order that genuine conversation can occur with the writer about the subject matter.

The character of this conversation in a given instance is largely unpredictable even though general patterns can be anticipated. Sometimes the conversation occurs at the level of historical explanation—we ask, in effect, why Amos did not mention the Ten Commandments or why Paul counseled paying taxes but did not remind the Romans of Jesus' words on the same theme (Rom. 13:1-7). The only way Paul or Amos can answer, of course, is by our further study. Sometimes it turns out that our question was misplaced; that is, the text itself corrects our line of inquiry. This is an important aspect of exegesis.

The Bible in the Pulpit

Given the cultural distance between ourselves and the text, and given the human penchant for hearing what we want to hear and filtering out the rest, the most important aspect of our conversation with the text is probing whether what it says is valid religiously and theologically. The range of questions evoked by the text has no known limit in scope or in time—*i.e.*, the meaning of the text continues to unfold as the conversation continues and moves from place to place. Take Paul's familiar assertion that three things last—faith, hope, and love, and that of these the greatest is love. Nothing in this statement is self-evidently true, even though we may have "believed" it for years. Why is it that just these three items abide? Does hope last as long as love? Why does not Paul, the greatest advocate of justification by faith, not say that faith is the greatest? Why is love greater than faith? Is this valid irrespective of the situation? If Paul is right, what difference does it make? A conversation over such questions leads not only back into the text (including the rest of Paul's work and its relation to the whole New Testament) but also into reflection about basic issues in theology and human experience. Once this process is set into motion, we find ourselves listening to the text in new ways, and usually to our surprise—and perhaps to our distress—we begin to understand it in a new way. Now the theme with which Paul wrestled is our theme too, and we discover that we share it with a host of others as well.

The outcome of this conversation cannot be predicted any more than its character. One might conclude that Paul or Amos was interesting but finally off base or naïve; one might conclude that the Johannine literature deals more profoundly with the same subject matter. Or one might discover that our previous ideas of faith, hope, and love were superficial (even though they were "meaningful" to us), and that a whole new vista has presented itself.

Underlying our reflections on exegesis as listening and conversing lies the axiom: we must take the text at least as seriously as we take ourselves. Whoever has learned to do this has learned to listen.

Whoever listens to the text and converses with it opens himself to the possibility that a word will be heard. This "hearing" goes beyond understanding. A word that is heard is compelling; it grasps us and our imagination; it causes us to reassess other words, values, and the web of assumptions and trusts that make up our lives. Such a word is not at our disposal like a commodity because it has elicited a response from our real selves. This is why exegesis as listening must not be confused with "taking" a text, nor with a preliminary exercise for sermon preparation. It is entering the danger zone where a word can happen to us. The person who has heard such a word can preach. Indeed, one must share it.

Second, although the process of listening and the event of hearing are accessible to everyone in principle, the preacher listens and hears as part of his or her office. The preacher listens for a word not only as a private citizen but as a representative of the church. The preacher's listening and hearing is a priestly act.

Because praying for people is a priestly act we understand, it is useful to compare this kind of praying with listening/hearing. It is, of course, much easier to pray over a congregation, to pray at them by using the prayer as a covert homily, or to make the congregation the object of prayer (praying about them), than it is to pray on their behalf. Our difficulties with intercessory prayer may explain why the so-called pastoral prayer is often the low point of the service. When I am invited to preach, I usually encourage a local person, the host pastor or a layperson, to offer the pastoral prayer, not because I am reluctant to pray in public, but because I find it exceedingly difficult to pray on behalf of people I have never seen before and may never see again. The genuinely pastoral prayer grows out of such intimate knowledge of the congregation that one can represent its deepest fears and highest aspirations, specious compromises and honest achievements, before God without faking it, or falling back on flowery generalities.

The pastor is truly a priest when the prayer articulates the situation of the congregation before God. Their lives come to speech through his or her prayer. For this to happen, one must listen to the people and establish a critical identity with them. No pastor can pray on behalf of the people if he or she regards them as obstacles to be overcome or as resources for new programs. To pray on their behalf, one must enter into their lives to the point that one begins to feel what they feel, yet without losing one's identity as a pastor. What is in view here is solidarity that does not obscure one's role and office, nor obliterate the capacity for critical judgment and distance. This critical identification is not peculiar to the ministry. Every counselor and social worker knows its demands. Developing this capacity takes time, and sometimes agony; I suspect that it may not develop at all if the preacher has never been grasped by a word that made him or her a responsible self with a clear identity.

Listening to the text is an analogous priestly act or process. Priestly listening means listening/hearing in solidarity with the people, vicariously; it is doing so on behalf of the congregation. In such a process, the word that he or she hears will speak to pastor and people simultaneously. The text will then not become a selected weapon against the congregation, a holy fulcrum by which one gets them to do or think as "they should." Rather, the text will be the listening-post where pastor and people together hear a word. Few things are more essential to biblical preaching than being aware that the word addresses pastor and people alike, that the struggle to appropriate the text is common to us all. The congregation soon senses when the preacher exempts himself from those to whom the text applies.

There is another aspect of priestly listening/hearing. Just as the preacher's own listening/hearing evokes questions, doubts, resistance, or hostility toward the text, so the congregation will respond in various ways. The vicarious listener knows what these responses are likely to be when he has genuine solidarity with the people, on the one hand, *and* when he is in sufficient touch with his humanity to be able to extrapolate from his own response, on the other. The conjunction of both elements is important. Extrapolating from one's own experience without having solidarity with the people leads to projecting one's own problems onto the congregation; purely vicarious listening/hearing (without involving one's selfhood) leads to manipulation of the text. The preacher's own humanness should not be withdrawn "for private use only" when one is listening/hearing the word through the text as a priestly act.

Exegesis for preaching, then, goes beyond understanding the text historically, indispensable as this is. Exegesis becomes fruitful for preaching when the text confronts the exegete, in solidarity with the congregation, with a word that intersects prevailing understandings and loyalties. Responses to this experienced intersection frequently are not pious; they often include bafflement, irritation, or resistance. Instead of feeling guilty about them, one should recognize them as signs that an issue has been located that needs to be worked through, as symptoms that a word is being heard. Out of this experience will emerge a sermon that is both exegetically grounded and eminently relevant because it was generated at the point of intersection. Such sermons have more power and relevance than those which draw three "lessons" and apply them. The latter type can scarcely avoid moralizing; furthermore, the text remains external to the human situation. The kind of sermon envisaged here, however, grows out of discovering the pertinence of the text; consequently in the sermon-making process the text and the present situation illumine each other throughout. A sermon that grows out of this experienced intersection does not put the text into the preacher's hands as a weapon (or as a bandage) to use on the congregation; rather it lets the text come through to everyone because the congregation was part of the listening and struggling with the text from the start.

Whereas the first two parts of the thesis pertain to the preacher's listening/hearing, the last two pertain to the preaching event itself. The *third* element concerns the way the experienced response to the text can function in the sermon itself. Just as the priestly prayer articulates the actual mind-set and situation of the congregation before God, so the sermon can articulate the perceived and anticipated reactions to the point of the text. In other words, the sermon can say out loud what we do not like to hear in the text.

What is in view here is an adaptation of the *diatribē* style used effectively by the Stoic street preachers in Paul's day, and by Paul himself. The Stoic preachers and teachers often wandered from place to place, addressing whomever they could in order to call people to a rational life free from passions, prejudice, and ignorance. In the markets, on the docks, in homes, these preachers developed a style of discourse in which they confronted the hearer directly and in which the hearer's response was formulated and taken up into the discourse as well. It is this feature of the *diatribē—*

the counter-question—which provides a useful prototype for effective biblical preaching. The *diatribē* must be adapted because frequently the counter-question, was formulated in a way as to be an artificial question, as if it came from a straight man who merely set up the next point. Still, Paul's own adaptation is suggestive.

In Romans 3, Paul brings to a head the first part of his exposition designed to show that no one attains a right relation to God by doing the works of the law (Rom. 3:20). At the end of chapter 2, he asserted that even for the Jew, what matters is not one's birth certificate but being a Jew inwardly, and that "real circumcision is a matter of the heart, spiritual, and not literal." Now comes a passage (Rom. 3:1-8) in which Paul writes in *diatribē* style.

Q: [If what matters is true, spiritual circumcision of the heart], then what advantage has the Jew? Or what is the value of [physical] circumcision?

A: Much in every way. To begin with, the Jews are entrusted with the oracles of God.

Q: What if some were unfaithful? Does their faithlessness nullify the faithfulness of God?

A: By no means! Let God be true though every man be false. *(Old Testament quotation follows.)*

Q: But if our wickedness serves to show the justice of God, what shall we say? That God is unjust to inflict his wrath on us? . . .

A: By no means! For then, how could God judge the world? [That is, such an argument implies that he ought to congratulate the sinner for bringing out God's justice.]

Q: But if through my falsehood God's truthfulness abounds to his glory, why am I still being condemned as a sinner? And why not do evil that good may come? . . .

A: [Because those who argue this way do not take God seriously,] their condemnation is just.

Q: What then? Are we Jews any better off?

A: No, not at all; for . . . all people, both Jews and Greeks, are under the power of sin.

Doubtless these counter-questions have a rhetorical character, just as it is likely that they distill Paul's frequent debates with Jews over the issues raised by the gospel. Consequently, this passage is all the more instructive for our reflection. By articulating these objections, garnered from experience and formulated trenchantly, Paul took seriously the readers' anticipated responses and acknowledged them openly. More than that, he used them to lead his thinking deeper into his own understanding of the matter.

In a similar way, today's preacher can articulate openly, and as trenchantly as possible, the anticipated (and known) responses of the people to the text and its theme. This will involve the congregation in the preaching act, and give the sermon a dynamic character as well—a dialogical quality without the artificiality that sometimes attends a "dialogue sermon."

Naturally, not every text lends itself to such a modern appropriation of the *diatribē*. Doubtless there are other ways to bring to expression in the sermon the resistance or surprise generated by the text. The point is that biblical preaching will be revitalized if the sermon is more, or other, than a weekly report of "what the Bible says," followed by several "applications" for today. If the sermon is more than a one-way discourse on biblical ideas and morals, it will engage the congregation on deeper levels than usual. Doubtless the word of God occurs through many forms and styles of preaching; still, some modes of discourse are probably more conducive to the happening of the word than others. A sermon that takes account of the people's reactions to the text and incorporates them into the discourse itself will be conducive to the occurring of the word among the people.

The *fourth* element concerns the prophetic witness of the

preacher. Once the sensed response of the congregation is articulated, the issue is joined. Now the preacher who has wrestled with the text until he or she has heard a word can change roles in order to become a prophetic spokesman on behalf of the text. In other words, the priestly role yields to the prophetic one, to that of a witness to the word that was heard through the text, especially as it may pertain to the responses that have been articulated.

Again Paul provides material for our reflection, though this time not an example of the shift of roles. In Romans 4:5 he speaks of God in a striking way, as the One "who justifies the ungodly." That is, God is the One who sets the impious in right relation to himself. This is one of the most radical understandings of God in the entire Bible, though no concordance would locate it because the word "God" is not used. But still, whoever hears the import of this text and announces it to the congregation can easily anticipate the response, for our entire scale of values, and much prevalent theology as well, is built on precisely the opposite understanding—that God is the One who justifies the godly and punishes the rest. Once this fundamental disagreement with the text is identified and made clear, the preacher who is grasped by Paul's insight can become a prophetic voice on its behalf—that is, on behalf of the God Paul is talking about.

This last element of the thesis makes it clear why exegesis demands more than acquiring information about the text, why it is important to penetrate it to the point where the exegete shares with the author the struggle to think through the subject matter itself. No one can speak prophetically on behalf of the text's understanding of the subject matter who has not grappled with the theme and been persuaded by the viability and vitality of how the text treats it. Likewise, it is now evident why the real self must engage the text and its author. The importance of historical critical exegesis should be equally evident—there must be some assurance that it is really Paul or Jeremiah who encounters the exegete person to person. This sort of exegesis calls for sustained work rather than sporadic attempts to read up on a passage.

The person who approaches the preaching aspect of the ministry in this way will not always strike a rich vein of ore; some passages yield their meaning only after years of study, brooding, and living with the subject matter. Likewise, the exegesis of life in our society will be the occasion when a particular text springs to mind as an insight missed before. All sorts of surprises can occur when the preacher takes the Bible seriously. Such preaching will lack neither vitality nor relevance. Above all, the congregation will share in the occurring of the word. That is the miracle of biblical preaching. When it happens, Lazarus will be unbound. He will show his face, and he will be articulate.

What has been delineated in this chapter is not peculiar to reading and interpreting the Bible. In principle, the same sort of process can occur with any significant text. The important thing, however, is that it does occur with respect to the Bible. What is special about the Bible is its relation to the church. What kind of Scripture does the church actually have? This question provides the agenda for the next chapter.

Chapter Three

The Bible in the Church

Effective biblical preaching requires an adequate understanding of both the content of the Bible, and the sort of Scripture it is. Both aspects of the matter are illumined by historical criticism. This chapter, however, will explore only the latter. One way historical criticism becomes fruitful for the preacher is by clarifying the Bible's relation to the church, where most preaching occurs.

Discussing the nature of the church's canon involves us in the theme, "the authority of the Bible." Traditionally, this topic has been dealt with in theological terms as part of the doctrines of revelation or of inspiration; that is, the authority of the Bible is derived from the self-revealing activity of God or of the nature of inspiration. The procedure here, however, will be different. We will remind ourselves of the kinds of literary phenomena found in the Bible, and of the church's role in the emergence of the Christian Scripture. We shall also see that attending to such considerations does not compete with confessional language about the Bible as the inspired Word of God. The aim of this chapter, then, is to overcome the impression that the Bible is an alien external authority over the church, and to help the minister see how his or her preaching has intrinsic continuity with the canon in the church.

The Thoroughly Historical Canon

The most important things are easily overlooked, largely because we take them for granted or else move them to the far edges of our memories. Only when something compels us to reexamine the whole structure do we become aware of the full force of what has been foundational all along. As far as the Bible is concerned, the forgotten or overlooked fact is that it has been canonized, declared to be the canon. The "historicity" of the Bible therefore means more than the claim that much of it narrates events whose historical character can be gauged; it means above all that the Bible is a historical event, subject to the sorts of contingencies and coincidences that characterize any history. The particular historical contingency that is in view here is the fact that it has been made the canon *of* the church *by* the church. This is so fundamental to the place of the Bible *in* the church that we must explore it briefly.

To begin with, although Christians and Jews have somewhat different Bibles, they agree in acknowledging that they themselves, as communities of faith, existed before their Scriptures did. Neither the faith of Judaism nor of Christianity is based on a book the way Mormonism is based on the *Book of Mormon,* or Christian Science is based on Mrs. Eddy's *Science and Health, with Key to the Scriptures.* The latter two religious communities would not have emerged at all apart from these two books. Not so Judaism and Christianity. Just as there was an Israelite community and faith before there was a Hebrew Bible, so there was a Christian faith and a Christian church before there was a New Testament.

The modern missionary situation must not confuse us. Nowadays the church emerges, say in Borneo, when people respond to the gospel that arrives simultaneously with the New Testament, which the missionary teaches, and frequently translates promptly. But originally it was not so. The earliest Christian missionaries, such as Paul, brought no New Testament to Corinth or Ephesus because there was no New Testament to bring. Nor did they introduce the Old Testament (as it was to be called later), for it was already there in the synagogues of the Greco-Roman world. Christianity did not emerge when someone arrived with a sacred book. Rather, it emerged in response to preaching the news of Jesus, which included a new way of reading the Scripture of the synagogue. The point is that the New Testament was produced within the church, which originally existed without it, and that the Old Testament likewise was produced in a religious community that had a long life without an authoritative text. One might say that today the Christian faith is based on the Bible because we have no direct access to the apostles' preaching, but this is only the result of historical development; in no case, however, must our situation be allowed to confuse the fundamental point—Christianity is not a response to a holy book.

Furthermore, both communities of faith remember that it was they themselves who determined what their Scriptures would contain and what would be excluded. (Naturally, in many cases only certain groups or persons in these communities actually remember this; the point does not depend on what a poll would reveal.) True, much of the story of how the Old Testament came to be canonized has been obscured and remains conjectural even today, just as it is impossible to reconstruct precisely the entire story of how the New Testament came to consist of just these twenty-seven books. The point is, however, that neither synagogue nor church has totally forgotten that they have the responsibility for what their Scriptures contain.

In the third place, Jews and Christians attribute the individual parts of their Bibles to particular historical persons. In other words, they remember "authors." The early church did not claim that God had dictated the Bible. We know that Hellenistic Jews told a legend about the miraculous translation of the Hebrew Bible into Greek (found in the Letter of Aristeas), but no such story circulated about the writing of either canon itself. Nor does any part of the Bible claim to be a heavenly deposit such as Joseph Smith claims to have found (the *Book of Mormon*). The closest we come to this is the apocalyptic books, only two of which (Daniel and Revelation) appear in the Christian Bible acknowledged by all churches (IV Ezra, or II Esdras, is an apocalytpic work in the Apocrypha, frequently called deutero-canonical in current Catholic thought). But even the Christian apocalypse names its author—John—an elder doubtless known to the original readers.

To be sure, historical criticism has revealed that both communities forgot more names than they remembered, and that in many cases their memories were faulty. For example, the name of the prophet whose work is contained in Isaiah 40–55 was forgotten once these materials were added to the book of Isaiah. Similarly, no one remembered who compiled Q, the sayings of Jesus used by the authors of the First and Third Gospels, just as only God knows who wrote the Epistle to the Hebrews. It is also clear that memory was more pious than accurate in attributing the Pentateuch to Moses, the Psalms to David, the book of Proverbs to Solomon, or in holding that the apostles Matthew and John wrote the Gospels that bear their names. Equally clear is the fact that some books got into the New Testament because the church accepted their claim to have been written by apostles, even though now it is apparent that someone else wrote them long afterward. Conversely, however, it must also be pointed out that some books did not get into the canon even though they did claim apostolic authorship or were attributed to apostles, because the church used additional criteria in the canonizing process. Fascinating as

the historical emergence of the canon is, we shall not pur-
sue it here because our concern is the import of there
having been such a process in the first place—both communities of faith associated parts of their Scripture with the
names of historical persons, not with angels or primeval
beings. In this context it does not matter whether the asso-
ciations can be validated by historical criticism or not;
rather, what matters is that the books were associated with
historical persons at all.

Whenever Christians lose sight of this fact, they inevitably slip into views of Scripture which are untenable historically and indefensible theologically. The Bible is not a
translation of a heaven-sent meteor. It is, as we shall see
shortly, a collection of writings anchored in history and
brought together into a canon by a thoroughly historical
process.

The conviction that the Bible is inspired does not compete with this fundamental historicity. "The inspiration of
the Bible" is an exceedingly complex topic once one gets
down to details and does not simply discuss generalizations. For example, would one be prepared to say
that the authors and compilers of literature otherwise lost
after being incorporated into present biblical books (Q, for
instance) were as inspired as the canonical authors who
used them? Was the composer of the secondary ending of
Mark, whose work is the basis for snake-handling
churches, as inspired as the Evangelist? These and similar
questions cannot, and need not, be discussed here. What
does need to be seen, however, is that one need not choose
between believing that the Bible is inspired and affirming
its full historicity. Three considerations should be borne in
mind.

First, to believe that Scripture is inspired is to believe
that particular historical persons wrote it under particular

circumstances. Had there been no memory of the historical origins of the biblical books, had there been only stories of direct divine intervention or of angelic mediation, there would be no need for a doctrine of inspiration in the first place. After all, a book dictated by God or delivered by angels has an inherent supernatural origin, and it would be superfluous to speak of the scribe who wrote it down as being inspired. What would that add? If anything, in such a case the appropriate word would not be "inspired" but "overwhelmed"—as Daniel 7:28 and 8:27 actually suggest (as do other apocalypses). It is true that II Timothy 3:16 writes of Scripture as "inbreathed" by God, but this is a view of inspiration more at home in Greco-Roman paganism than in the rest of the Bible. Nor should it be forgotten that although Paul reports that he had been "carried away" by the Spirit into the third heaven, not a line of his Epistles claims to repeat what he had seen or heard in such an inspired state. Even the author of II Timothy 3:16 does not claim he himself is inspired, for he is thinking of the Old Testament, which was his Scripture.

Second, to believe that the Scripture is inspired is to make a confession of faith—that through this literature the word of God occurs in a special way. The confession accounts for this occurrence by pointing away from the person who hears the word, in order to make it clear that the word is not self-generated. We speak of the inspiration of the Bible in order to acknowledge its power and to link it with God.

Third, it is most important to see that when we speak of the inspiration of the Bible, we are not explaining anything in the Bible or about the Bible on the historical level. Inspiration-language does not function on the level of historical explanation at all, because historical explanations have to do with causes and effects. Inspiration does not explain why or how Matthew used Mark, or how the book of Isaiah came to contain what it does. Inspiration accounts for one's experience with the Bible in terms of God's action; to that extent it is an explanation. But this "explanation" is, as we saw, a confession of faith. Because God is the Ground of all causes and effects and not one of a series of causes, it is theologically improper to make God a cause in historical explanation. In explaining things historically, one can appeal to belief in inspiration as a historical cause, but not to inspiration itself. "Inspiration" belongs to another mode of discourse.

Since the Bible is a thoroughly historical canon, it is entirely appropriate to understand it by means of historical criticism. Our next task, therefore, is to bring into focus the ways in which the Bible is the church's creation from start to finish.

The Canon as the Church's Creation

This section of the chapter does not intend to summarize the historical processes by which sixty-six books came to constitute the Protestant Bible. The basic information is readily available in books devoted to the subject, in critical Introductions to the Old and New Testaments, and in articles in Bible dictionaries, such as *The Interpreter's Dictionary of the Bible*. Our aim, rather, is to remind ourselves of salient matters in order to show the extent to which the Bible is the creation of the church. Primary attention will be given to the New Testament, where I am more at home; an adequate discussion of the Old Testament canon would enrich but not change drastically the point being made here.

First, however, a preliminary remark is in order with respect to the Bibles we read. In the first chapter we noted in passing that the fundamentalist preoccupation with the autographs—the original manuscripts of a given biblical book—is misplaced because there is no autograph to read. To that observation we add another: it is fundamentally wrong to regard biblical criticism as a threat to the Bible, because it is biblical criticism that has given us the Bibles we actually do read. Every Bible we can read rests on someone's judgment about what the right wording is. This is as true of Hebrew and Greek Bibles as it is of any version. Even if we read photostatic copies of the oldest and apparently most reliable manuscripts (this judgment itself is a critical one!), we are reading a text that someone deemed to have the right wording; indeed, the manuscripts themselves contain corrections in wording, written in the margins or over the lines. True, frequently errors crept into the text by accident; at other times the copyist thought he was correcting a mistake when in fact he was creating one. But precisely this phenomenon shows that wording of the Bible depended on someone's judgment almost from the start. Scientific text criticism can be regarded as an accelleration of the same fundamental process of making judgments about the text, a process made necessary by the existence of many manuscripts that differ considerably among themselves, on the one hand, and made possible by the development of coherent principles of criticism on the other. Every Bible embodies a critical judgment about its wording. Even the most bitter foe of biblical criticism relies on the critics' work whenever he or she quotes a single line of the Bible.

For our purpose, it is useful to distinguish four stages in the development of the Bible as we know it, even though there is considerable overlapping:

Stage 4:   canonization
      3:   adaptation for community use

2: creation of the literature
1: antecedent traditions and texts

We shall look at them briefly, beginning with the latest stage.

The *fourth* stage—canonization—was a long and complex process whose rate of speed differed from place to place. Moreover, we must distinguish the canonizing of the Old Testament from that of the New. It is generally held that the Hebrew canon received its definitive form around 90 C.E. by the decision of the rabbis who assembled at Jamnia (Jabneh). Ascertaining the extent to which they largely ratified what had already come to be authoritative in the synagogues need not delay us here. What does interest us is two aspects of the Christian adoption of the synagogue Bible as part of the Christian Scripture.

First, although first-century Christians took for granted that the synagogue Bible was their Scripture too, the second-century church had to fight to keep it. It was in the middle years of the second century that the first radical reformer of the church appeared—Marcion. He undertook to purify the church of its Jewish elements because he was convinced that Jesus came to save humanity from Judaism and its God, the creator and law-giver. Marcion therefore insisted that the church jettison the synagogue Bible and develop its own specifically Christian Bible instead. He argued that this should consist of the Gospel of Luke and the Letters of Paul (from both of which he deleted passages favorable to the Old Testament; he believed that he was removing additions that had been made by "Judaisers"). Marcion's phenomenal success was a major threat, for he persuaded many congregations, some of which persisted in Marcionism for several centuries. The church responded by insisting that it could not surrender the Old Testament without forfeiting the gospel. The Christian Bible contains the synagogue Bible not by default but by deliberate decision.

Second, Christians have never been able to agree on exactly what constitutes "the Old Testament" they retained. The problem was inherited because the Greek-speaking synagogues had not defined their own canon by New Testament times. The Septuagint was not only a translation of the Hebrew Bible but also an expansion of it, for it contained additions to books like Daniel and Jeremiah, and whole books not found in the Hebrew canon, such as the Wisdom of Solomon. Later, the Septuagint was translated into Latin; in 1546 the Council of Trent defined the Old Testament canon in such a way as to include this additional material (which Protestants call the Apocrypha). The Reformed churches, on the other hand, rejected these books and accepted only the Hebrew canon, as defined by the group at Jamnia. The Church of England neither accepted the Apocrypha nor rejected it, but reduced it to second-class status—as books that are good and useful but that lack authority sufficient to base doctrine upon. It was common to print Protestant Bibles with the Apocrypha between the Testaments. Had this practice continued, there might never have arisen the nonsense about "four hundred years of silence" between the Testaments (from Malachi to Matthew). Today, one can buy a Bible with or without the Apocrypha, or an Apocrypha without a Bible.

Few things manifest more vividly the church's role in creating its canon than the story of its attempts to define what the Old Testament contains. It is unfortunate that so little of this story is part of common Christian consciousness.

Marcion's role was pivotal also in the canonization of the New Testament. On the one hand, by limiting his canon to

Luke and Paul he provoked the church into expanding its canon. It would have four Gospels and the Letters of more than one apostle; the church's canon would be catholic, not sectarian. On the other hand, the church adopted the structure of Marcion's canon: a Gospel part followed by an Epistle part. The church modified this by inserting Acts as a connecting link (even though this meant separating Volume Two from Volume One, Luke), and by adding, eventually, an apocalypse—the Revelation to John. The oldest list of twenty-seven books that corresponds to the New Testament as we know it comes from the letter of Bishop Athanasius, written in A.D. 367. But it would be centuries before such a list would be acknowledged everywhere.

"Canonization" can be defined in various ways. To some writers it means acceptance of a book for use in public worship and instruction; for others it means formal adoption as authoritative by a duly acknowledged church council or leader. Although the latter meaning is preferable, canonization does not mean initiating a new status for literature; it means officially recognizing a status that it had acquired by use in the church. Canonization also means refusing to acknowledge other literature as Scripture; it sets limits to what can be tolerated as an authority. Canonizing also means "making normative," as the etymology of the word suggests. That is, in canonizing certain writings, the church acknowledged them to be a norm of faith and life, a criterion by which it would gauge its fidelity. In creating its canon, the church subjected itself to these writings as a standard.

What sort of norm did the church subject itself to? In the first place, the norm is not what is oldest. That is, the New Testament is not simply a collection of the oldest Christian literature even though it contains it. The latest book in the canon is commonly dated around A.D. 150 (II Peter). If we look at the total literary production up to this time, it is immediately apparent that what is in the New Testament is but a fragment of the whole. By the third century there were many gospels, epistles, "acts," and apocalypses. The New Testament is not at all the archives of earliest Christian literature but a deliberate selection from it.

In the second place, it is not a representative collection either, because many segments of early Christianity are not represented at all. For example, although much of the material in the four Gospels originated in Palestine, we have no document in the New Testament that represents that form of Christianity which developed under the leadership of James in Jerusalem (the Epistle of James was written elsewhere by another James). Nor does the New Testament contain any book that speaks for those Christians who hated Paul; to the contrary, it is a very pro-Pauline collection, since more writings are linked with his name than with any other apostle and the latter part of Acts is clearly presenting Paul in a favorable light. In other words, the New Testament is a highly selective anthology made by the church across many centuries.

The details of the *third* stage—adaptation for community use—are even more elusive than for the fourth. Moreover, the fourth stage did not replace the third, but can be regarded as a special phase of it because the adaptation process was going on before, alongside of, and after the canonizing process. One thinks, for example, of the copying of manuscripts for reading in church, or of the compilation of lectionaries. Nonetheless, what is in view here is the history of the text between the time it was written (stage 2) and its canonization. What happened to this literature as it came to be used in the churches? We must bear in mind that the church canonized not manuscripts but books, and the books that were canonized were not necessarily identical in all respects with the originals. By the time a book was canonized its text had incorporated those changes which had occurred in the course of its use in the church. The more sophisticated research methods become, the more we are able to retrace this history and its effects on the text. This is why text criticism is more than a matter of comparing manuscripts and determining their genealogies in order to posit the most likely original wording; it also includes accounting for the differences in the wording, and that means relating these differences to the history of the church. Text criticism is part of church history, and of the history of Israel/Judaism as well, because the texts have histories within the histories of these communities.

A few examples may make the matter concrete. (a) Sometimes a writing was combined with one or more other documents in order to produce a fundamentally new work. Thus the Yahwist's history (and the Elohist material associated with it) was combined with the Deuteronomist's material and with the priestly traditions of Israel in order to produce a new work which, in turn, came to be divided into five books known as the Pentateuch. Likewise, Mark and Q were combined with other materials in order to produce Matthew and Luke. (b) Sometimes a given work attracted a variety of materials across the years, so that what we have is a highly complex anthology that no one planned at the beginning. One thinks of the prophetic books, such as Isaiah or Jeremiah. Sometimes pieces were combined. Thus II Corinthians is really a compilation of at least four letters of Paul, none of which was used in its entirety. (c) Sometimes minor additions were made to books after they received their basic form. For instance, the Song of the Men in the Fiery Furnace was added to the Greek version of Daniel, Mark was given two later endings, and John received an appendix (chapter 21). As we saw, Marcion thought that Luke and the Letters of Paul had been changed so drastically by this process of addition that he undertook to correct the text by subtracting the later elements. He was aware of how the text had been transmitted; but he was too committed to a rigid theological position to be able to understand Paul, so he subtracted the wrong sections.

There is no need to extend this list of things that befell the literature as it was used in the church. The point is clear: the exact original form in which Hebrew and Christian writers produced their works is irretrievably lost; what we have are those forms of their writings which have come down to us—as used and edited by the synagogue and church and other communities (*e.g.,* the commune at Qumran). Gradually some of this literature being adapted for community use came to be canonized, but this did not stop the changes, for variations in wording continue to appear, and sometimes in content as well (*e.g.,* the story of the woman taken in adultery was added to some manuscripts of John, at different places, and in a few instances to Luke).

Probably it is the *second* stage—the author's writing the book or letter—which has gotten the major attention of biblical criticism. Here too the community's role was decisive, although this was not always given its due because the legacy of romanticism focused attention on the creativity of the writer as an individual. For our purpose the main point is that essentially the Bible is a collection of occasional literature. "Occasional" does not mean sporadic, nor written for special occasions (though this is true for some of the Psalms); rather, here "occasional" means "occasioned by." That is, the books of the Bible were elicited by particular occasions or situations in the life of the communities of faith. The literature of the Bible was written in the community, for the community, and by a member (or members) of the community. It is "in-group" literature. Again, we need but remind ourselves of what every critical Introduction to the Old and New Testaments has already taught us.

With regard to the New Testament, it has been claimed from time to time that some of its books were written not for the Christian communities but for outsiders. For instance, it has been asserted that John and Hebrews were missionary pieces, designed to convert the readers to the Christian faith, and that Acts was intended to elicit a positive response toward Paul on the part of a hostile government official. Yet these claims cannot be supported adequately. The books in question contain too many intramural interests, matters of concern only to Christians. Nor were the New Testament books written to be sold on the open market, in the book stalls of the Hellenistic cities. The New Testament does not bring together literature written "to whom it may concern." Apart from III John and Philemon, it does not contain private correspondence either; the Pastorals have merely been made to appear this way. They too were written for the churches. The New Testament literature is thoroughly church literature at the moment of its creation.

Nowhere is the occasional character of the New Testament books more apparent than in the letters of Paul. Paul regarded his letters as substitutes for his own presence in his congregations (except for Romans, of course). He wrote when he could not pay a personal visit to deal with problems directly. Moreover, he knew that his letters would be read aloud to the congregation; it would be a long time before anyone read silently. Therefore he dictated as if he were speaking to the church; it is not surprising, then, that we find rhetorical devices, such as the *diatribē*; in his letters (see the previous chapter). When the letter was read aloud, Paul would in effect be "speaking" to the church. The letters are the written form of what Paul would have said to the church had he been on the scene.

Furthermore, Paul did not drop his letters into the mail, so to speak, but sent them by courier. It is highly probable that the courier himself read the letter to the congregation, just as we are justified in thinking that he would feel free to comment on the contents as he went along—perhaps pointing out what Paul regarded as of special importance, or fleshing out details of a rather compressed style. In this way Paul's letters were texts for preaching and teaching from the start. He intended that they function this way, and took this into account when he dictated them.

Analogously, the Gospels too were intended to be used in the churches, though it is impossible to prove that their structure reflects their use as Christian counterparts to the lectionary use of the Old Testament in the church, as has been suggested. Nonetheless, it is clear that the Gospels order and interpret the Jesus-traditions for the benefit of the churches. How much of a given Gospel was read on a single occasion we do not know; doubtless it was a much larger portion than is customary in the church today, for nowadays a congregation almost never hears any Gospel read through. That aspect of biblical criticism which has emphasized the intimate relationship between problems of the churches and the Gospels as they stand is redaction criticism, developed after World War II. However, it must not be overlooked that the modern era of New Testament criticism began with F. C. Baur (in the first half of the nineteenth century), who correlated each writing with a particular stage (and group) in the history of early Christianity. Although few scholars today agree with Baur's particular conclusions, they all understand every book to be a response to concrete occasions in the life of the churches.

With regard to the Old Testament, the situation is more complex but not basically different. The complexity is greater partly because the books were produced across a much longer time span, and partly because some of the Wisdom materials and Song of Songs may have been generated primarily out of the creative impulses of gifted individuals instead of being produced for community use at the outset. Still, when all this is taken into account, the tapestry is richer and more varied, but the broad design is the same: the books of this part of the Bible too were generated by particular occasions in the life of the community.

Increasingly, it appears that it was during the Exile that particular groups created the books we know, using older traditions and texts to do so (*e.g.,* the Pentateuch was created by priestly writers adding their distinctive version to the combined Yahwist-Elohist-Deuteronomist materials). We must not think of such groups as archivists primarily bent upon preserving records of the past. Rather, they created the present books (whether Pentateuch or Prophets) out of older materials for the sake of the exiles and later the returnees. Likewise, wherever one locates in time or place the "wisdom schools," one should not regard their products as conventicle literature (as at Qumran); it too was produced for the sake of the larger community of faith and practice.

The *first* stage lies behind the writing of the biblical books. Biblical criticism has expended a prodigious amount of effort in the attempt to "get behind" the texts to the authors' sources and traditions; in fact, nineteenth-century criticism was preoccupied with the question of sources—earlier documents—that may have been used by the writers of the Pentateuch or the Gospels. Despite excesses, the results of this work remain foundational for most biblical study today; it taught us to detect the

Yahwist's account within the Pentateuch, the strong probability that Matthew and Luke used Mark and a collection of Jesus' sayings that we label Q; recently source analysis has established the likelihood that one of the literary sources of John was a "Signs Source."

Form criticism taught us to look for the orally transmitted traditions that lay behind the written sources (and alongside them) that the authors used, and to detect their functions in the life of the community. Later, concern for the function was extended to the written books themselves. In other words, form criticism has sensitized us to the function of the material in the community; it has called our attention to ways in which community usage has shaped the material. The fundamental dictum is, "Form follows function." By analyzing the form, we can infer the function. In principle, this can be done with every biblical book and all its antecedents. Indeed, there may soon be published a form critical commentary on the entire Old Testament. On the New Testament side, although form criticism was first applied to the Synoptics, it has also been used effectively on Acts and the Epistles. Unfortunately, relatively little form criticism has been done so far on the Apocrypha.

It is not necessary to rehearse the manifold results of form critical work on the Bible. What matters is seeing the result: the writers of the Bible adopted and adapted material that had been transmitted in their communities, sometimes for long periods of time. Just how much of a given biblical book, when it was first read, was new to the original hearers of it differs from book to book, and in most cases can no longer be determined. Sometimes the content may have been largely new to a given audience although it may have been known to other groups in the community as a whole. For example, we do not know whether the readers of Luke already knew Mark, which was one of its sources; perhaps the book of Judges made available to all Israel the stories of local tribal heroes which had been known previously to only individual tribes; probably the Philippians had sung (or chanted) the Christ-hymn that Paul quotes in Philippians 2:5-11. Whatever the individual case may have been, the general point holds—much of the biblical material had been known in the communities of faith and practice long before it was taken up by the author and written down into the text we have (or into written sources he may have used).

Exploring the prehistory of the text also includes the quest for the antecedent history of its ideas, motifs, or practices. Whereas text, literary (source), redaction and form criticisms have concentrated on the text and its forerunners, the "history of religions" approach has investigated ideas and practices which are assumed, mentioned or expounded in the text. It is here especially that archaeological finds have been vital, especially for Old Testament study. The more we have been able to trace parallels and antecedents of biblical ideas and practices, the more it turns out that what was once thought to be distinctive of the Bible was not at all unique at the time. Scholars no longer, fortunately, write simply of "borrowing" from Canaanite religion or from Stoicism. Today, the sensitive interpreter discerns both what is shared and what is rejected from the cultural environment. It must not be forgotten that whereas today's critic might be able to trace a motif in the Bible through its prebiblical antecedents and parallels, often to remote antiquity, the biblical author himself probably did not know where the idea or practice came from, and might not have cared if he had known it. For us, however, this knowledge is important. For one thing, it keeps us from equating evidence for revelation with what strikes us as unique in the Bible; such a stance puts the content of revelation at the mercy of the next excavation because the more parallels and antecedents are discovered, the less revelation is left. Furthermore, it compels us to rethink fundamentally what we mean when we speak of the revelation of God in and through the Bible.

We have reminded ourselves, swiftly and tersely, of the four stages in the making of the Bible in order to emphasize that the Bible is the church's book (if one may extend "church" to include the parent community, Israel/Judaism) all along the line. What remains to be done in this section is to reflect on the import of this fact for biblical preaching.

First of all, the Bible is not an external authority imposed on the church against its wishes from outside the church. To be sure, particular areas of the ancient church resisted the inclusion of certain New Testament books in the canon, just as churches that adhered to the Westminster Confession later refused to acknowledge the Apocrypha as inspired and authoritative. The point, however, is that no one compelled the church as a whole to accept or reject the canon we have. The canon was created by the church. The authority of the Bible is distinguishable from that of the church, but not isolable from it. The authority of a particular canon reaches no farther than that of the church that canonized it. For instance, were the Pope (or some future Vatican III) to canonize the Gospel of Thomas, with its 114 sayings attributed to Jesus, most Protestants would probably refuse to accept it. Conversely, even if a group of Protestant churches were to add the 151st Psalm (found at Qumran) to the Psalter, other communions would probably decline it. The canon is as open or as closed as a given church agrees to make it, and is able to enforce its decision. In other words, there is no compelling historical or theological reason why the church could not change the canon;

there are, however, significant "political" reasons why this cannot be undertaken in the foreseeable future.

Second, there can be no more talk of a fundamental contrast between Scripture and Tradition because it has become evident how much of Scripture is itself tradition, not only oral tradition "behind the text" but also the traditional role of the book which the church canonized. In other words, the church canonized part of its tradition, but this process did not obliterate the "tradition-character" of what was now canonical. Biblical criticism has helped to send the Reformation/Counter-Reformation battle over Scripture or Tradition vs. Scripture and Tradition to the dead-letter office.

Third, to preach a Bible so thoroughly rooted, at all levels of its development, in the church is to carry forward the inherent intentionality of the literature. When the Bible is preached, it is not undergoing a strange experience, being used in ways essentially alien to itself or shoved into foreign contexts. Rather, it is letting the literature come through in its native habitat. The same cannot be said for preaching from the plot of a novel or a movie or, for that matter, from an anthology of religious literature garnered from the corners of the earth—irrespective of how informing, stimulating, and inspiring such sermons can be.

Fourth, biblical preaching puts the congregation in touch with its own heritage. The biblical writers, compilers, and editors, as well as copyists and canonizers, are our elder brothers, not alien authorities over us. Bible preaching transmits the family story handed down from remote times, and so prevents the amnesia we mentioned before. To preach the Bible is to claim and transmit our own legacy. Of course, a preacher will find formative material for a given sermon in all sorts of other places. But the real question is whether, over a period of time, the congregation is made conscious of its continuity with a community of faith that reaches back to Abraham and Sarah. Biblical preaching is part of consciousness raising, for without consciousness of continuity with the whole church and its predecessor (and sister), the synagogue, the congregation degenerates into a religious society or cult designed to meet the needs of its momentary clientele. That is no longer church.

If the Bible is the literature produced in the church for the church and later canonized by the church, is then the Bible simply the literary precipitate of the church? Is the Bible, then, ultimately nothing other than the canonized ideology of the church? Does not the church's affirmation about divine inspiration of the Bible really amount to the claim that the church stands securely on divinely authorized warrants? That would indeed follow were the whole story told. In fact, however, only half of it has come into view. The other half must be brought into view next.

The Canon as the Church's Critic

Form criticism has made it clear *that* traditions are used in the biblical literature, and redaction criticism is exploring *how* how they function in a given text. It is the redaction-critical insight that will be pursued here. Put simply, the writers often used church traditions against the church. The Bible is not only the church's product, but an anti-church book at the same time. It is the interplay between these two elements that makes the Bible the kind of canon it is. "Anti-church" does not mean sheer hostility, but a trenchant critique of the church as it was actually developing. In short, what the church canonized as the New Testament was a series of twenty-seven minority reports.

To be sure, we do not know whether the canonizers

represented the majority or the minority of Christians at a given time and place; in all likelihood they did represent the actual power structure, and so regarded themselves as standing in continuity with the literature they canonized. (The extent to which they may have been right, at least more right than the alternatives at the time, is a matter we need not explore here.) Canonization is really not imaginable had they thought otherwise. Orthodoxy always regards itself as the guardian of the continuous Christian tradition going back to Jesus and the apostles. Therefore it regularly regards itself as the arbiter of "correct" interpretation. In practice, this usually involves harmonizing differences between one book and another, making an appropriate place for disparate materials within an overarching scheme or category, neutralizing the palpable criticisms of the church in the text by restricting them to localized abuses during the writer's own time, and minimizing differences between orthodoxy's current position and that of the canon.

A personal experience crystalizes what is in view. In 1963, after the World Council of Churches convened in Montreal, I participated in a week-long meeting of New Testament scholars representing the member churches of the Council, as well as Roman Catholics. This ecumenical group studied and talked amiably enough—until the last day, when things came to a head. A representative of the Orthodox Church (not identical with "orthodoxy" of course) had enough of the Protestant view. Waving his New Testament in our faces, he said, "In the name of this book you disrupted our churches in India and elsewhere. How can you criticize the Body of Christ in the name of this book? To be sure, Paul is critical of this or that blemish in Corinth, but it is not possible that he would have criticized fundamentally the church itself." With that, the fat was in the fire. Young Turk as I was, I rose to argue that, to the contrary, what Paul saw going on in Corinth was jeopardizing the authenticity of the gospel and the integrity of the church at the most elemental level, and that by no means could one regard his critique of Corinthian church as a matter of simply smoothing out a few wrinkles.

In the long run, it does not really matter how the ecclesiastical establishment thought it was related to the text it was canonizing, because it has become evident that what it canonized does in fact repeatedly criticize the established church of the moment. It is not accidental that ecclesiastical structures of power reacted vigorously and defensively to the rise of biblical criticism, and sometimes still do, for it is biblical criticism that repeatedly calls into question the presumed continuity between the church of today and the New Testament on the one hand, and the validity of the church's harmonizing of the diverse canon on the other. Indeed, if biblical criticism is bankrupt, as Walter Wink charged (see p. 28), it is because it has made its peace with the church too soon.

The critical dimension of the biblical literature is discernible at each of the four stages we traced in the previous section. Showing this, however, would expand this discussion inordinately because one would need to probe lesser known aspects of the history of the canon, and in some cases place the development in a rather broad context to show what the issues were at each stage. That research needs to be done, but in another context. We shall, instead, concentrate our attention on that stage where the critical aspect is most evident and most important for the preacher—the writing of the literature (stage 2). We shall first note how pervasive was the critical function at the time the biblical books were written, then how the writers used traditions in carrying out their objectives.

Manifestly, Paul is the clearest instance in the New Testament. Had his churches been as trouble-free as Acts implies (in Acts, all problems for Paul are generated by outsiders, never by his own churches), he would not have written most of the letters we know. He wrote so often to Corinth (at least four times) because the situation there kept deteriorating. What Paul deals with in his letters to Philippi, Thessalonika, Corinth, Galatia are developments within his own churches which he regards as fundamental threats to the gospel. Paul's letters are therefore critiques of what was going on in his own churches during his absence. Even Romans, being sent to a church Paul had not yet seen, reveals his attempt to arrest current trends there, which surface in chapters 14-15. Paul did not write in order to express himself or to develop an aspect of his personality that was not tapped otherwise— the way some persons write poetry late at night, when the day's work is done. He wrote, rather, in order to confront trends in his churches with a trenchant critique, grounded in the cross/resurrection of Jesus.

Other parts of the New Testament are no less critical of what was going on in the churches. That the Johannine Epistles address tendencies toward distortion is clear, for I John regards the "heretics" as the Antichrist, and III John reveals a crisis in leadership. Given the growing importance of the sacraments, especially the Eucharist, by the end of the first century, some interpreters have regarded the Fourth Gospel as critical of sacramentalism because it replaces the Lord's Supper with the Last Supper, from which the words of institution are absent. Moreover, John 14:26 regards the work of the Spirit-Paraclete as making pertinent the memory of Jesus; this suggests that the Evangelist is contending with a tendency to regard the work of the Spirit as virtually surpassing the importance of the once-upon-a-time event of Jesus.

It has become clear that Mark struggles against a Christology that magnifies Jesus the miracle-worker. Mark deals with this by emphasizing the fact that the more miracles the disciples see, the less they understand, and by showing that a right understanding of who Jesus is comes only in light of the cross and in the experience of one's own discipleship. Matthew's Gospel deals with a church that thinks its fate is secure because its Christology is correct; so he not only emphasizes the coming Judgment but insists that on that day there will be surprises for everyone—especially for those who now say, "Lord, Lord." For each of these Evangelists the situation at hand is utterly serious, and cannot be corrected by an exhortation to try a little harder to live up to the Christian ideal. The fidelity of the church and the integrity of the gospel are at stake. This is why the New Testament literature has a polemical edge, one designed to cut into the church as it was actually developing at the time.

Doubtless many of the original readers did not perceive their situation in the same terms. We know that Paul's readers in Corinth did not. They were alienated, at least at first, by what Paul had written. How one would like to have been present when his letters to Corinth were read there for the first time! But how different was it when Mark was first read? Or Matthew, John, James, or the Apocalypse? We delude ourselves if we suppose that the first readers greeted each new work as a gift from heaven, for which they could not help giving thanks. The New Testament embodies a struggle within the church for authentic faith and faithful life. This is why New Testament Christianity must not be confused with early Christianity; in fact, Christianity according to the New Testament is a fundamental critique of the early Christianity that actually was developing.

Precisely the same point must be made for much of the Old Testament. Old Testament faith and religion is not the same as Israelite faith and religion, but a series of critiques of it. Had the religion of Israel been on course, there would have been no occasion for an Amos to speak out at Bethel, for a Jeremiah to preach on the temple steps. The prophets who merely expressed the religion of Israel and reassured their hearers that the ship was on course are not the ones we remember as "the Old Testament prophets." Likewise, the Deuteronomistic history is more than a literary precipitate of Israelite religion and tradition; it is rather prophecy in the historical mode. The story of Jonah confronts the people with a call to fulfill its destiny among the nations, as does Deutero-Isaiah. The Wisdom literature might easily be regarded as a critique of nation-based faith and ethics, inasmuch as it virtually ignores the theology of the convenant (except in later Wisdom books that bring these motifs together). The one major book in the Old Testament that can scarcely be considered as a critique of Israelite faith and theology is the Psalter.

In developing their critiques of their communities, the biblical writers commonly drew on the community's own traditions. The writers did not merely record them nor did they simply copy older written materials. Each author or group (as is likely with regard to some Old Testament books) selected, ordered, and reshaped the traditions (and texts) in order to make the point.

An instructive example of this procedure is provided by the book of Judges. Here the old traditions of the various tribal heroes are taken up and put into a comprehensive narrative whose theme is clear: after Israel became faithless to Yahweh and adopted Canaanitish ways, oppressors appeared; in due course, God "raised up" X or Y, who led the people in revolt. Then follow the traditional stories of the individual "judges"; then comes a formula conclusion that X or Y judged Israel for so many years. Then the cycle repeated itself. In this book, one can easily distinguish the tribal traditions from the framework, just as in a stone wall one can distinguish the stones from the mortar that holds them in place. So in the book of Judges, the wall is the work of the redactor/author, whereas the stones are the traditions and complexes of traditions of the several judges. The author/editor used the materials not merely to preserve them for posterity but to confront the community with his word: Be faithful, or this pattern will repeat itself again.

The Gospel writers too were not merely transcribers of church traditions about Jesus, but pastoral theologians whose ordering and shaping of the material were designed to confront their churches with a critical word. As noted, for instance, Mark was critical of the tendency to regard Jesus as a miracle-worker, a "divine man" of which his culture had an ample supply. He did not reject the miracle stories, but used them in such a way that their limitations became apparent; *i.e.*, he put them into a context in which they were balanced by the call to follow the Jesus who bore a cross. Matthew did not simply copy Mark, but rearranged it at certain places, and inserted and arranged the Q material (plus other traditions) in order to create a wholly new work; this is characterized by five discourses, each of which ends with Jesus' word about the Judgment, which faces even the church.

Not only narrative books reveal this critical use of tradition, but also the Epistles. Repeatedly Paul used common church traditions in order to deal critically and correctively with problems in his churches. In discussing ethical questions at Philippi, for instance, he confronted the church with the import of a Christ-hymn that it probably knew long before (Philippians 2). Faced wth a distorted view of resurrection, Paul confronted the church in Corinth with a tradition that he himself had received and transmitted to them (I Cor. 15:3-11), and then upacked its logic in such a way as to show that the trend in Corinth actually contradicted what the Corinthians had accepted as foundational. Paul used a similar procedure in addressing abuses of the Eucharist. In Colossians the Christ-hymn in 1:13-20 is the basis for dealing with the problems at Colossae. The deutero-Pauline letters show that Paul's theology has itself become authoritative tradition, at least for some, and so the authors of Ephesians, II Thessalonians, and the Pastorals articulate this Pauline tradition critically into their own situation by writing in his name.

Only the most obvious instances have been cited because a full discussion of this aspect of the Bible is not necessary to make the point. Most scholarly Introductions to the Old and New Testaments contain the material, even though it is not identified as supporting evidence for the critical aspect of the literature. In other words, what is commonly discussed as the "occasion" and "purpose" of the book has been interpreted here as a situation that the writer regarded as a crisis of faith and practice, one that he addressed critically by selecting, ordering, and interpreting materials that his community already acknowledged. The procedure is akin to that of Martin Luther King, who confronted the American people with their basic text—the Constitution—and thereby exposed the contradiction between the norm and the actual state of affairs in order to move us toward fidelity to what is authentically American.

It would be foolish to think that one could color-code the Bible in such a way as to identify which parts are critical of the church and which parts are supportive of it. For one thing, some literature addresses situations that have not reached crisis proportions and that do not elicit critiques of the church from the writer. Hebrews, for instance, is written to a church whose problem is spiritual fatigue, and Romans sought to allay fears of Paul before he himself arrived on the scene. Moreover, the books were seldom written with just one aim in view. The Gospels, after all, are narratives about Jesus' mission and identity, not epistolary expositions of doctrine; it would be very short-sighted to reduce the Evangelists' aims to correcting particular trends in their churches. Besides, a piece of tradition, or a text, that has a particular function in one context may well have another function in the next. What matters is seeing that there is a church-critical dimension to the New Testament.

What evoked the writing of a given biblical book must be inferred from the book itself; likewise, the writers' resources—oral and written—must also be inferred (only twice does Paul tell the readers that he is quoting; I Cor. 11:23; 15:3). It is inevitable therefore that diverse proposals and hypotheses should be advanced, many of which appear to cancel one another out. The busy preacher cannot be expected to master all the proposals and counter proposals. What can be expected, however, is an overall working framework within which the many parts find their place, at least provisionally. Reconstructing the situations and the resources of the writers is very much historical knowledge, and in both senses; it is not only about a slice of contingent history, but is itself contingent knowledge, seldom stable and always provisional and probable, subject to revision. There is no reason why this should debilitate or inhibit the preacher. Rather, it should free him or her from the anxiety that if one does not "get it right" all is lost. In biblical interpretation, as in any other interpretation, there are no "correct" answers at the back of the book. There are only "answers" with varying degrees of plausibility and probability. In this regard, biblical preaching is no more and no less vulnerable than any other kind of preaching.

Historical criticism may have deprived us of innocence about the Bible, but at the same time it showed us that the Bible is the end product of a living and vital tradition repeatedly interacting with the community in which it was produced. At almost every point, the biblical literature is multilayered. The text embodies stages through which traditions have passed, and the printed versions in use today represent a continuation of this intimate and intricate interaction between the community and its Scripture. The Bible is both the creation of the church and its relentless critic.

The point, in other words, of emphasizing the church-critical dimension of the New Testament, and of the Old Testament as well, is to counterweight the perennial tendency on the part of the church to regard the Bible almost solely as its warrant. It is that. But it is also the church's most incisive critic. This is why every reformation of the church is accompanied by, and often energized by, a rediscovery of the Bible as a prophetic protest against the prevailing state of affairs. This is also why biblical preaching is the most dangerous form of preaching that a church can hear or a preacher undertake.

If we have gotten an outline of the kind of canon the church has, and if the Bible itself is the criterion of what makes preaching biblical, then we are ready to proceed to the next chapter, in which our observations are related directly to the preaching task.

Chapter Four

When Preaching Becomes Biblical

The renewal of biblical preaching requires us to find an alternative to moralizing. It is hard to conceive of any mode of preaching more deadly to the hearer or more inimical to the Bible itself than the prevailing pattern of drawing lessons for today from a text that has been explained briefly. This is not to deny the importance of explaining the text, even less of the need to correlate it with the situation of the congregation. What matters is the way in which the text is related to the hearers. If the Bible is the criterion of biblical preaching, then that correlation must accord with the Bible itself. Moralizing "application" of the text is a markedly unbiblical way of preaching the Bible.

Before seeing what the alternative might be, it is useful to clarify what is meant by "moralizing application" and to indicate why it violates the character of the Bible itself.

Farewell to Moralizing

Every preacher wants to make the Bible relevant if he or she uses it at all. This impulse manifests both a pastoral concern and on occasion a prophetic passion as well. Moreover, the more aware one becomes of the way in which the biblical literature is imbedded in antiquity, where cultural and intellectual assumptions fundamentally different from those of our own time prevailed, the less one wants to simply repeat or paraphrase the biblical content. That would make the congregations into bystanders or onlookers as the biblical content was being described. I recall hearing an Advent sermon that was a classical example of this: "Paul's Idea of Messiahship." Although basically accurate, it was really a lecture that described Paul's ideas and left everyone wondering, So what? It is precisely sensitivity to the "So what?" question that prompts preachers to move as quickly as possible from the text to its contemporary application.

All too often, however, this impulse is so strong that the preacher does not deal seriously enough with the text to be able to relate it to the present. The sermon actually imparts the ideas and concerns that the text may have triggered in the preacher's mind. A phrase, a metaphor, a feature of a story, simply serves as a catalyst; the actual content of the sermon is derived elsewhere and frequently could have been suggested just as well by a fortune cookie. How often, for instance, has the parable of the prodigal son produced sermons on the importance of self-discovery, which were triggered by the line, "When he came to himself . . ."! Such a sermon, sound as it might be from other angles, does not make the text relevant, but actually makes it irrelevant. As implied in chapter 2, the Bible becomes relevant only when the preacher takes the text with utmost seriousness. In most cases, moralizing applications manifest a fundamental failure at precisely this point.

Moralizing means drawing moral inferences, usually things to do or become. A moralizing sermon can have a "soft sell" (suggestions for better living) or a "hard sell" (obligations to be met or prohibitions to be observed). A moralizing sermon can allegorize the text ("a pearl of great price" can become any virtue worth attaining by sacrifice) or it can formulate a principle that is then applied to life (the merchant who bought the one pearl was resolute; hence we need to be resolute with regard to X, Y, and Z). Moralizing sermons invariably emphasize things to be done, virtues to be developed, or even beliefs to be held.

Now there is no doubt that the Bible itself emphasizes the importance of human action, indeed moral action. The demand for righteousness pervades the Old Testament just as the call to faithful discipleship, or life appropriate to being in Christ, is fundamental to the New. Christianity, like its parent, Judaism, is an intensely moral religion, deeply concerned for the shape of life in this world. Nor is there any doubt that congregations need to be confronted with the ethical and moral meaning of the Christian faith. What is decisive, however, is whether this is done in a way that accords with the Bible's own way of understanding moral obligation.

Several considerations will show why moralizing sermons distort the Bible, whether they are simply set in motion by something in the text or whether they deal more thoroughly with it. First of all, moralizing has the effect of transforming the Bible into an assortment of moral precepts and examples. The Bible's own agenda is replaced. Where moralizing prevails, the congregation is cheated out of the Bible's own overarching concerns, such as the election of Israel, God's commitment to establishing justice on earth (most moralizing sermons are oriented to individuals), the meaning of Christ as the fulfillment of the Old Testament, the kingdom of God and the call to repentance, or the eschatological horizon of human existence. Moralizing frustrates the Bible as the coherent disclosure of the ways of God to which human life is called to respond. Frequently, moralizing either treats the Bible as the basis of advice as if it were reducible to the book of Proverbs or to a collection of exemplary hero stories, or it treats the Bible as the warrant for a rather narrow and often parochial morality. The Bible's own way of thinking is sidetracked. Inevitably, the Bible becomes an uninteresting book, an incoherent jumble of materials that, in a highly inefficient way, contain general moral truths.

In the second place, moralizing distorts the historical reality and concreteness that characterize the Bible because it idealizes the past in a way that the Bible usually does not. This occurs especially with regard to the early church or to individual apostles such as Paul. Far too often, sermons portray the early Christians as if they were the real Christians, as if everyone afterward—with some notable exceptions like Luther, Wesley, or Bonhoeffer—were at best a pale carbon of the real thing. Again and again sermons tell us that in the early church, faith was pure, love pervasive, prayers effective, courage dauntless, and the presence of the Spirit warmed every heart. We are told such things because we are urged to be like the early Christians. Actually, of course, we are already more like the early Christians than we ought to be.

Christianity according to the New Testament is not the Christianity of the early church, but a trenchant critique of it, as we saw. (Conversely, moralizing often uses Israel as a negative example to be avoided, so that the early Christians wear white hats and the ancient Israelites black hats.) Biblical figures are more significant for preaching precisely when they are not lionized but portrayed in proportions with which the hearers can identify. The heroic achievements of the prophets and apostles can and should be articulated in the pulpit; in a day when the Christian community generally lacks models for Christian trust and style, biographical sermons are quite in order. What matters is whether the portrait is credible, and how the hearers are related to it. Where the prophets and apostles are idealized the hearer will either suspect that the truth has been suppressed for propaganda purposes, or conclude that "such knowledge is too wonderful for me; . . . I cannot attain it."

In the third place most moralizing sermons distort the Bible's own understanding of moral obligation. To put it into traditional Protestant words, they obscure the proper relation of law and gospel. Clearly this is not the place to work through that complex theme or even to identify all the issues. Suffice it to say, however, that in the Old Testament no less than in the New, law is God's gift so that human obedience is a response to God. Most moralizing reverses this and makes God the respondent of human achievement because it subtly makes "God" the guarantor of the rewards of virtue, the patron of achievement. Theological clarity at this point is especially important when one preaches from the Sermon on the Mount. All too frequently, the Sermon is sundered from the context into which Matthew placed it—Jesus' announcement that the Kingdom is at hand and the consequent call to respond by repentance (turning life toward the God who is coming as King). For both Jesus and Matthew, the demands of the sermon are the concretions of repentance to what God's grace is doing— bringing the Kingdom *so that* persons may change. Jesus brought the Kingdom near not to those who by achievement had met minimum requirements, but to those who had not done so, so that they might. Moralizing invariably extracts the demands of Jesus from their total context of his mission and thereby treats them as autonomous moral obligations or ideals for those who want to "do what's right." From such preaching the gospel has fled.

Finally, moralizing assumes that the fundamental task of the sermon is to tell people what they should be or do. Indeed, there is a place for this emphasis, as noted above. But surely constriction occurs when such preaching becomes the prevailing pattern. Cumulatively, such preaching forfeits the capacity to celebrate God's grace, to illumine the enigmas of life and death, or to connect the histories of the people with the history of the People of God. The preacher ceases to be a vehicle through which the Bible confronts the people in its richness and power; instead he or she manages, and probably manipulates, the impingement of the Bible on human life, for now the preacher is in control of what is relevant. The result tends to be either a distressing trivialization of the Bible into reasonable advice for individuals, or a shrill demanding of absolutes for the church and society. Moralizing sermons do not trust the congregation to appropriate the Bible, nor do they develop the people's capacity to see for themselves how the text impinges on their lives. The priestly listening discussed in chapter 2 does not lead to moralizing; actually repeated moralizing would eventually preclude priestly listening. In fact, habitual moralizing debilitates the preacher as a sensitive pastor and theologian.

In short, moralizing has got to go! It ruins the preacher, it obscures the gospel, it distorts the history of biblical groups and communities, and it inhibits the Bible from coming through on its own terms. There has got to be a better way.

Preaching the Bible Biblically

Before developing the alternative to moralizing application, it is useful to pull together certain major themes that have been discussed. We began by saying that the Bible itself is the criterion for what makes preaching biblical. This criterion, it turns out, is a library of mostly multilayered literature, the end product of a long and complex history spanning more than a dozen centuries, affected by many cultures and written in three languages for communities of faith in a great variety of situations. It is a thoroughly historical norm. This criterion is the written distillate of living traditions, and at the same time these traditions are frequently used to criticize the very communities that transmitted them, and to summon these communities to a mode of life that is appropriate to authentic faith.

Biblical preaching will be renewed when the two elements of the word "biblical" are given their due—that is, preaching is truly biblical when (a) the Bible governs the content of the sermon and when (b) the function of the sermon is analogous to that of the text. In other words, preaching is biblical when it imparts a Bible-shaped word in a Bible-like way. Historical critical exegesis is an indispensable tool for truly biblical preaching because it illumines both the biblical content and its function. The paragraphs that follow will explicate this understanding of the matter. It would be foolish to claim, of course, that this is the only valid understanding of biblical preaching. It is, however, one valid way of approaching the matter, and I believe it is viable enough to advocate.

Biblical content as criterion. Preaching is biblical when the Bible is preached, not simply preached about. In other words, the first sense in which the Bible is the criterion or canon of preaching focuses on the content of the sermon. Clearly, the Bible can become the content, or shape the content of the sermon only if the preacher takes the text seriously and exegetes it carefully. Everything discussed in chapter 2 about hearing/listening is important for just this reason, as are the remarks made in the previous section of this chapter with respect to sermons that merely are occasioned by something in the text. The Bible can be preached only if it is understood and affirmed. When that occurs, the preacher becomes the medium through which the biblical message reaches today's hearers.

There are several aspects of the biblical content that merit comment. First, articulating and interpreting the biblical content is vital to the self-understanding of the congregation because the Bible is the decisive thing that links a particular congregation with the whole church across milennia and miles. The New Testament is the only thing all Christians share, and, apart from the Apocrypha, they are agreed on the Old Testament as well, which in turn links Christians to Jews. Where the Bible's message is preached, the congregation is invited to appropriate (not merely affirm) its meaning, and so identify itself with the biblical faith and the world church. Despite the fact that the interpretation of the Bible has divided Christians, the ironic fact is that they are linked to one another precisely by the common text on which they continue to differ.

In the second place, to preach the content is to preach diverse accents. The unity of the Bible is not uniformity in theology but constancy of perspective. Its unity is more like that of a highly individuated and sometimes quarrelsome family than that of a disciplined, ideologically uniform political party. Preaching the Bible must reflect this pluralism. Preaching ceases to be biblical if it blends this diversity into a V-8 juice theology. This blending occurs when, for example, the text is from Paul but the sermon itself is Johannine, or when the incarnation is read into Mark, or Paul's understanding of faith is confused with that of Hebrews. There are, to be sure, overarching convictions that all New Testament writers share (or would not repudiate), such as the centrality of Jesus Christ, the presence of the Spirit, the necessity of reading the Old Testament through the lens of Jesus and vice versa, the expectation of Christ coming in glory, or the church as a community based on faith and baptism and not on ethnic identity. These themes, and others, provide the family resemblance of all the parts. Nonetheless, it is a fundamental task of exegesis to identify the specific and particular content that each writer gives to these themes so that, for example, Paul is not confused with anyone else, including those who wrote in his name. Preaching the New Testament responsibly requires one to respect precisely these differences without exaggerating them.

By evermore bringing the distinctiveness of each writer's work into view, historical exegesis has actually enriched the possibilities for preaching the biblical content. On the one hand, it is insufficiently appreciated that it is historical criticism which has freed us from the eighteenth-century embarrassment of having to deal with "contradictions in the Bible." Debunkers, then and now, have always had a field day pointing out everything from historical discrepancies to theological incompatibilities because, like their orthodox opponents, they assume that the Bible is valid only if it is both error-free in all respects and theologically self-consistent at all points. The whole argument is off base. Diversity, inconsistency, and occasional factual errors are precisely what one must expect in a book that came into existence the way the Bible did. The logical tensions and historical inaccuracies are a threat only if one assumes that the religious and moral power of the Bible depends on demonstrating that these differences do not really exist. The more one learns to appropriate historical criticism, the freer one is from the compulsion to make the diverse pieces of the Bible fit into a single jigsaw puzzle. On the other hand, by the same token, one discovers that this diversity multiplies the insights and so increases the possibilities for preaching the Bible as a polychrome tapestry instead of a monochrome etching. As we shall see presently, it is precisely because the Bible's literature was addressed to different situations that its diversity enriches the possibility for hearing in it a word for diverse situations today. Wherever the differences are obscured, to say nothing of being denied, there the text is not being taken seriously, just as a person is not being taken seriously if his or her individuality is not respected. Preaching the content of the Bible faithfully requires one to respect the peculiarities of a given text or writer, even if—or should we say, in order that?—this means that the emphasis of this Sunday's sermon from Romans will have certain tensions with last Sunday's from Matthew. Respecting the diversity, particularity, and limitations of each writer frees one from the compulsion to make any given text say everything that is true, and allows the preacher to expound the gospel more fully across the span of time because no biblical writer put the whole truth into writing.

The diversity and mutual tensions in the biblical literature appear nowhere more clearly than in the Gospels. The preacher often wishes that there were but one account instead of four that cannot be harmonized—even though tradition does this at Christmas by having the wise men appear shortly after the shepherds, and on Good Friday by constructing the seven last words. Apart from the fundamental divergence of John from the Synoptics, even among the latter the same basic saying of Jesus is sometimes reported so differently that one is often uncertain how to end a sentence that begins, "As Jesus said. . . ." Moreover, the same incident is sometimes reported in one context by Mark and in a quite different setting by Luke (*e.g.*, the story of Jesus preaching in Nazareth, Mark 6; Luke 4). When one is sensitive to the plot of each Gospel, one sees that a given incident takes on different significance because each evangelist has reported, and placed, it differently from the others (*e.g.*, the story of Peter and Jesus at Caesarea-Philippi; Matthew 16, Mark 8, Luke 9).

Redaction criticism has accounted for many of the differences in the treatment of the same material; each Evangelist shaped it to serve his aim, and form criticism has illumined the character of the orally transmitted tradition. Thus we can often trace the history of the material through several stages: the situation of Jesus (if it is a genuine saying or a historically probable event), the oral tradition, Mark, Matthew's use of Mark, and Luke's use of Mark.

If one is to preach such material the preacher must make some decisions. The historical question (Did Jesus really say this, and if so which wording is most likely to be an accurate rendering of the Aramaic? Did this really happen?) is crucial primarily if one decides to preach from the stage of Jesus himself. However, the historical question is not crucial if one decides that the sermon will emerge from a later stage, from the text as it stands, for then what matters is that the particular Evangelist's presentation be understood and preached as a version of the gospel. In principle, where the same material is found in all three Synoptists, four sermons are possible: one from each of the Evangelist's treatment and one that focuses on Jesus in his situation. The possibilities vary from case to case, depending on whether each Evangelist's interpretation is sufficiently distinctive to merit a separate sermon. But the point is that far from depriving the preacher of material for preaching from the Gospels, biblical criticism actually provides more possibilities than most preachers care to take advantage of.

Exploiting the potential of the Synoptics for preaching requires careful and sustained work, and using the *Gospel Parallels*[1] is presupposed. Moreover, one must engage in sustained study of the individual Gospels as literary and theological works, not simply as scrapbooks containing the memorabilia of Jesus. The Matthean interpretation of the Good News can be articulated, for instance, only if the preacher is informed of Matthew's theology as a whole; otherwise one will read from Matthew and preach Luke without knowing the difference. The new commentary series being published by Fortress Press is a welcome tool for preachers;[2] likewise, Eduard Schweizer's commentaries on Matthew and Mark are designed to aid preachers in discerning each Evangelist's Gospel.[3]

In the third place, preaching the biblical content leads one to face a whole range of issues in interpretation. This is because preaching the Bible requires interpreting it, specifying what it means, translating its language and assumptions into an idiom that is both appropriate and adequate. In one way or another, probably every preacher has struggled with these questions. Missionary Bible translators have long been sensitive to these matters, exemplified in the problem of translating the Twenty-third Psalm for people who never saw sheep. Actually, all interpretation is translation (and vice versa of course)— transporting the idea expressed in one idiom to another. Every translator knows that one cannot translate perfectly, that one must risk paraphrase, that some nuances have no equivalent in the receptor language, that in the process something is frequently lost and that sometimes the translation creates ambiguities and difficulties not anticipated by the translator. Each of these aspects of translation is found also in the interpretation of ideas. Hebrew *nephesh* is not really identical with Greek *psyche* or English soul, nor is Torah equatable with *nomos,* or law; nor is *teshubah* identical with *metanoia, poenitentia,* or repentance. Furthermore, given the pervasive secularization of our own culture, many persons no longer understand even the English Bible. Terms like "regeneration," "incarnation," "covenant," "grace," or "savior" no longer convey their biblical meaning, just as "love," "spirit," "peace," or "sin" readily impart meanings that are not adequately biblical. Whoever wants to preach the Bible, continually struggles to find ways of conveying the message couched in such terms.

This is not the place to work through the subtle and complex matters involved in the interpretative process, nor in the character of language. It must suffice to offer three comments.

One thing to be said is that the interpretative work has different levels. On the simplest level, it is a matter of explaining terms and concepts such as those mentioned. On this level the interpreter's task is to provide accurate information, such as why the Bible speaks of going "up to Jerusalem" even when people are traveling southward. On this explanatory level the preacher functions as an educator, or guide to biblical antiquity; the aim is to make the text intelligible so that it can be understood more precisely. On another level, the interpreter seeks modern equivalents for biblical terms. For instance, Clarence Jordan's *Cotton Patch* translation uses "The God Movement" for the kingdom of God, and some theologians have found it useful to speak of God as the power of the future, or the whence and the whither of human existence. On this level, one substitutes meaning-equivalents for verbal or semantic equivalents. On the third level, the interpreter engages in what Bultmann, somewhat misleadingly, called demythologizing. Here one asks for the religious/existential meaning that is expressed in mythological language, such as the Last Judgment, the Ascension, and the like. Bultmann insisted that such language must be interpreted, that the real meaning is to be found "behind" such concepts and terms lest one make the mistake of thinking that this language describes divine action. Actually, for Bultmann it expresses something about human existence in relation to God, and it is that which must be discerned and made clear. Bultmann's proposal failed to win the day, partly because he relied on existentialist categories to formulate the meaning behind the biblical language and those categories themselves have proved to be inadequate, and partly because his view of myth has turned out to be problematic. Nonetheless, Bultmann's instincts were sound, and most preachers demythologize in one way or another even if they do not have a word for what they are doing or use the one Bultmann offered. In any case, the point to be made here is that it is better to run the risks of demythologizing than of moralizing, because the former takes the text seriously and strives to find a way of letting it say what counts.

A second thing to be said is that the hermeneutics—understood as principles of interpretation—generally emerge after the fact. Rarely, if ever, can one prescribe in advance how a text must be interpreted. There is an intuitive, imaginative, venturesome, spontaneous quality to all interpretation. One suspects that Bultmann's demythologizing proposal failed also because it tended to be prescriptive, to dictate in advance what one could and could not legitimately hear in the text. Be that as it may, it appears that for most creative interpreters the meaning of the text seems somewhat self-evident because that meaning is found by discernment and insight rather than by applying principles or following rules of interpretation. Such an interpreter might not at all be able to answer readily the question, By what principles did you arrive at that meaning? Only in retrospect does it become clear what was going on in the interpretive process, and even then it is usually someone else who sees the operating principles more clearly than the interpreter does. Even when the interpreter becomes self-aware of the process, it is often in retrospect, after one has done it repeatedly. Bultmann, after all, demythologized long before he formulated the principles. The point of this observation is not to discourage pondering the principles of interpretation or attempting to work consistently. Rather, it is to encourage preachers to study their sermons in order to discover and assess the patterns or principles of interpretation by which they may have been preaching. Critcial self-assessment is, after all, a key element in being professional.

The final comment on the interpretative process is the rather simple observation that the move from understanding what the text meant to what it may mean, from historical, descriptive exegesis to proclamation, need not be made in the pulpit. That is, one need not devote half the sermon to describing the original meaning and then resay it for today. That interpretative move must be made, but in many cases it must be made in the study rather than in the pulpit. The danger of doing both tasks in the pulpit is that one ends up laying a ten-minute lecture next to a ten-minute sermon, neither of which is satisfactory.

Having looked at various aspects of preaching the content of the Bible, we now consider certain dimensions of doing so biblically, of doing so in a way that accords with the function of the content in the Bible itself. How does one preach the Bible in the biblical way, in a manner that accords with the biblical precedent?

Biblical precedent as criterion. The central motif to be explored briefly is this: what the biblical writers did belongs as much to the criterion of biblical preaching as what they wrote. It is at this point that the previous chapter's observation about the Bible being an anti-church book becomes pertinent to the preaching event today. What the biblical writers did cannot, of course, be reduced to their critical intent, but that is a major component and it must be recovered. The point is that one is faithful to the Bible not simply when one imparts its message-content, but only when one does so in a manner that repeats the Bible's own way of using normative tradition. It is precisely at this point that especially redaction criticism becomes fruitful for preaching. Indeed, what has been noted about the whole New Testament, and most of the Old, becomes decisive for preaching—that this is occasional literature, written in response to particular occasions (usually crisis situations) in the life of the communities of faith.

Unless this is borne in mind, one easily slips into thinking that he or she is preaching from an anthology of timeless truths, a compend of religious and moral materials that are rooted nowhere in particular. Then one ends up applying timeless principles and abstractions to concrete situations today. One might preach effectively, and might even impart accurately biblical ideas, but one would not be preaching in a biblical way. To preach biblically is to take full account of the concrete issues to which the text was addressed in the first place; it is to reckon with the fact that what the biblical writers found necessary to say was determined not by truth in general but by needs in particular. The situation of the community, as perceived by the writer, set the agenda, and the traditions provided some of the resources for addressing it; the text is a selected and focused truth in the form of a literary response.

In exploring this dimension of biblical preaching we shall again look at the matter from several angles. First, whereas the heremeneutical task of imparting the biblical meaning is focused on the content of the text, the hermeneutical issue here focuses on the way one correlates the original readers and today's readers. There we reflected on the hermeneutics of the content, here we focus on the hermeneutics of the recipients, then and now. The preacher must identify what today's hearers share with the authors' original readers so that the text confronts them both. When this happens, the event of the text repeats itself; just as I Corinthians confronted the Christians in Corinth with Paul's word (including his reinterpretation of the tradition they had already acknowledged, according to I Cor. 15:1-11), so the sermon becomes the vehicle through which Paul's words confront today's congregation.

Congregations will not know themselves confronted unless it becomes clear that they are modern Corinthians, for instance. Here too, what was said previously about idealizing the early Christians must be borne in mind. Idealizing the early Christians has the effect of obscuring precisely the necessary similarities between today's churches and those of the first century. Conversely, the more sharply one focuses the image of the early Christians, whose wayward discipleship and propensity for misunderstanding evoked the New Testament, the more readily one discerns parallels between then and now. Preaching that emerges from the awareness of these continuities will not "apply" the text to life today; rather, it will communicate the discovery of its pertinence because today's church is already addressed along with the original readers.

Discerning the continuities between today's church and that of the New Testament (or of Israel and the Old Testament) complements what was said before about the continuity of the church, and does so in two respects. First, by imparting the biblical content, the preacher fosters the role of the Bible as normative tradition. Unless the church is conscious of the Bible as a norm, any subsequent appeal to conform to the biblical word will fall flat. There is simply no leverage in proclaiming "what the Bible says" if the hearers do not regard the Bible to be important to them. In other words, just as Mark or Paul could summon their readers to authentic faith by confronting them with acknowledged traditions, so the preacher today can be effective in his or her appeal to the Bible only if its content has become imbedded in the church as an acknowledged norm. To put it still differently, the second aspect of biblical preaching being explored here—precedent as criterion—depends on the first, content as criterion. If congregations are to understand themselves to be accountable to the Bible, and if the biblical content is to have any moral valence in the church, the content must be implanted in the church's consciousness. Otherwise one cannot do effectively with the biblical tradition what the biblical writers themselves did. That is, one cannot preach the Bible biblically, but only in a moralistic way.

Second, whereas preaching the content of the Bible generates a continuity of the church by means of a common text, the continuities between today's church and that of the New Testament, which are our concern just now, are a given because certain perversions of life and of Christian faith are perennial, paradigmatic; indeed one may even call them archetypal. This dimension of the matter is never seen by moralizing preaching from the Bible. To be sure, a moralizing sermon may well urge people not to be like the scribes and Pharisees whom Jesus criticizes. Fair enough—except that a moralizing sermon is always heard as "Do not become like them," whereas the type of biblical preaching being advocated recognizes that there are important ways in which we are already like the scribes and Pharisees, so that Jesus' criticism of them strikes us as well, and calls today's scribes to repentance just as it did those of yesteryear.

The hermeneutical task of preaching the Bible in a way that is biblical, then, requires theological analysis and interpretation of today's hearers, and the same categories must be used at both ends of the arc. For example, preaching from Galatians means understanding the Judaizers and their appeal in Galatia; unless the problem generated by this movement is clarified, Paul's answer makes little sense or becomes a theological treatise abstracted from concrete reality. But preaching Galatians biblically also requires one to locate today's "Judaizers" and their appeal in today's churches. Obviously, these are not people who want to make the church more conscious of its sister faith, modern Judaism; nor are they Christians who have their newborn sons circumcized. Rather, once one sees that in Paul's day the Judaizers were demanding that gentile Christian men be circumcized if they wanted to be first-class, bona fide Christians, then we can see that theologically "circumcision" is any required act that is supposed to supplement trust in Jesus as the sole requirement for a right relation to God and to God's people. Then one can see how often "Galatianism" appears in our churches, and Paul's word will be as pungent a confrontation with the gospel today as it was then—and it might generate the same sort of resistance.

Third, if the preacher exposes the theological/moral continuity between today's congregation and the original readers to whom the text was addressed, then he or she occupies a position analogous to that of the writer. In other words, as text was to original readers, so the preacher is to today's congregation. At first glance this is a rather ego-building position in which to be—just like Paul or Amos! In fact, however, it is such a precarious place to be that we cannot avoid reflecting further on this matter.

For one thing, the discussion of priestly listening (chapter 2) emphasized the need for critical solidarity with the hearers lest the preacher exempt himself or herself from those whom the text addresses and so use the text as a club on the congregation. That observation is especially germane here, lest one assume at the outset that "of course" the preacher is on the side of the biblical writer. The preacher must, in fact, be there if he or she is to articulate, interpret, and advocate the writer's point; however, one should not take it for granted that what the text says pertains only to the congregation. When preaching from the Gospels, it is important to remember that sociologically, and perhaps theologically as well, the preacher is the scribe and the Pharisee—the professional interpreter who is always in danger of using exegetical knowhow to protect himself or herself from the impact of the text.

Preaching that focuses the attention on the present to elicit a mid-course correction is a prophetic act, for it does the same sort of thing that Amos or Paul did. Because "prophetic" is an adjective most preachers cherish for their ministry, including their preaching, it is useful to recall that preaching in the prophetic mode involves love and compassion for those addressed. If prophetic preaching is not motivated by and infused with love it becomes harsh and scolding. When this is the case, what is actually communicated is animosity, or one's own moral superiority, or one's own alienation from "the system." It is fortunate that there is a cadre of preachers who have increasing sophistication and insight into the church's bondage to culture, and an understanding of the ways in which that bondage distorts Christian faith and hence calls for a prophetic word. What is *un*fortunate is that this insight engenders a sense of superiority to and alienation from the person who thinks evangelism is the church's top priority, or from those who do not believe that one must ever choose between loyalty to the American flag and loyalty to Christ. Truly prophetic preaching, at least as exemplified by biblical prophets, struggles to combine clear insight with deep compassion for those who do not yet see what the preacher has seen, and who may never see it at all. Precisely when the preacher sees things more clearly (if indeed he or she does!), it is the preacher who bears the responsibility for not jeopardizing the insight because of his or her own personal alienation. Amos not only delivered the word at Bethel but prayed on Israel's behalf, "How can Jacob stand, for he is small?" Paul not only wrote trenchant critical letters but agonized over his churches. In a word, just as preaching love without truth becomes chatter, so preaching the truth without love becomes a shrill voice of alienation. Whoever wants to preach prophetically must earn the moral right to do so by compassionate critical solidarity with those addressed. It is not enough to be right.

Another thing worth pondering is that doing a prophet-like or apostle-like thing with the biblical tradition will probably lead to a clash over the interpretation of the Bible. After all, the congregation being addressed critically may also appeal to the Bible in support of its understanding of Christian faith and life. In fact, it might be precisely the prevailing interpretation of the Bible that is at the root of the problem that the preacher wishes to address. This was, by analogy, the case when Jeremiah preached his sermon on the temple steps, when Jesus said, "You have heard . . . but I say to you," and when Paul found it necessary to correct the abuses of the supper in Corinth. The Corinthians were doubtless surprised to read, "It is not the Lord's Supper that you eat" (I Cor. 11:20)—*they* certainly thought that it was.

The probability of a clash of interpretations puts special obligations on the preacher. Not only must one know the content of the Bible thoroughly, but one also needs to be aware of the history of its interpretation. It is often helpful to be able to show that what people regard as the self-evident meaning of the Bible is in fact a particular mode of interpreting it that emerged at a particular time. For example, the idea that the kingdom of God is the rule of God in the individual heart, that it has to do primarily with the relation between the soul and God, arose in nineteenth century Protestantism under the influence of Schleiermacher, who emphasized the sense of dependence on God as the center of religious sensibility. More important, the preacher must be able to defend his or her interpretation by explicating it theologically, and by contrasting it with the implications of the alternative that one is trying to replace. Unless one is able to do this, one simply falls back on one's own authority, either conferred by ordination or acquired by superior education. Such a strategy might silence the objections but it will scarcely persuade.

Historical thinking helps the preacher put not only the prevailing interpretation of the Bible into perspective and so deprive it of its self-evident correctness, but it also helps one to deal with certain parts of the Bible that have created much mischief in the church. Not everything in the Bible is theologically sound or morally binding just because it is in the Bible. One thinks, for example, of Paul's confused arguments by which he tried to support the view that women should wear veils in church (I Cor. 11:2-16); even he senses that none of his arguments go anywhere and so he simply falls back on his authority and precedent (v. 16). Or, one thinks of I Corinthians 14:34-36, which forbids women to speak in church, and requires those who wish to know something to ask their husbands at home (leaving no option for the unmarried woman). It is highly likely that this passage was inserted here by someone who agreed with I Timothy 2:11-12, written by a Paulinist. Such considerations may salvage Paul's reputation among women, but the content of the passages in question must itself be

assessed theologically and morally, and in light of the perceived center of the gospel and of the canon.

Whoever undertakes to preach the Bible biblically discovers that the biblical precedent for handling the tradition
calls for the responsible exercise of freedom. Not only do
New Testament writers interpret the Old Testament with
striking originality (and sometimes with what strikes us as
ingenuity), but Matthew and Luke have little hesitation in
changing Mark (just as the tradition did not refrain from
attributing sayings to Jesus and doubtless forgot some of
the things he did say), nor is Paul afraid to reinterpret Jesus'
sayings about divorce. Later the Synoptists did the same
thing; according to Mark 10:2-4, Jesus rules out divorce, but
according to vv. 10-12 (introduced by the typical Markan
device of giving private explanations of public preaching),
Jesus is interpreted as being concerned with avoiding adultery caused by remarriage, and, in accord with Roman law,
recognizes the right of the woman to divorce the
husband—something Jesus himself did not have to face.
Likewise, Paul recognizes that Jesus did not approve of
divorce, but then, also in accord with Roman law, adds, "if
she does [divorce]" she should either not remarry or be
reconciled with her former husband. Equally important,
Paul had to face the question of "mixed marriage"—
something Jesus never had to deal with—and so extrapo-
lates from the tradition what he believes is sound counsel.
When faced with the question of whether people should
marry at all, he recognizes that here there is no "command
of the Lord" to go by, but nonetheless ventures his own
judgment (I Corinthians 7).

This New Testament treatment of divorce is an instructive precedent. Not only do we see the writers struggling to
be faithful to the word of Jesus while at the same time
taking account of the actualities of their own situation, but

we see them claim their freedom by avoiding a literal, legalistic application of Jesus' words. What Jesus said is not the end of the matter but the beginning, so to speak. In fact most of the problems faced by Paul had not been faced by Jesus and the Palestinian church—which may be one reason why so few of Jesus' words appear in Paul's letters, which were evoked by pastoral problems. In any case, Paul, like today's preacher, sought to articulate the import of the inherited tradition into a culturally different situation where new issues arose. Being faithful to Paul therefore involves more than repeating what he said and then relating that legalistically to current situations. It also calls for claiming Paul's gospel-given freedom to do as he did. We are not faithful to the New Testament if we decline to share the freedom and responsibility of its writers. The only way to keep faith with the free and responsible interpreter is to claim that freedom and responsibility ourselves, to see ourselves as persons doing the same sort of thing in our day as they did in theirs—even if this means saying somewhat different things. Precisely in the matter of divorce, one must take account of the different view of marriage in the contemporary world, and above all consider whether God has in fact joined together any couple that goes through the marriage ceremony; and whether, in those cases where the persons have never become "one" and probably never will, one is not more faithful to Jesus by encouraging divorce than by sticking to the letter of his words.

The diversity of the New Testament documents suggests that there is no single way of exercising one's freedom to interpret the Christian tradition responsibly. Nor does the New Testament say that the preacher is always right, or indeed that he or she must be. Indeed, because preaching the Bible participates in what Paul calls prophecy (I Corinthians 14), the sermon is subject to assessment by the hearers. Development of talk-back sessions is in accord with Paul's meaning. This does not compromise the authority of the preacher, still less that of scripture or the word of God which may occur through the sermon; rather it includes the congregation in the process of struggling to hear the word through the text and does so in a way that is both faithful to the gospel and germane to the hearers.

We may conclude these reflections on the dual dimensions of biblical preaching—preaching the Bible's content and doing so in a way that comports with what the biblical writers themselves were doing—by observing that when biblical preaching is undertaken in this way, it can be rewarding for pastor and people alike. The preacher himself will inevitably be involved in an enterprise that produces continued growth, not only in understanding and interpreting the Bible, but also in interpreting the situation of the people. One cannot engage in biblical preaching as sketched here without coming to terms with the root questions of faith/theology, of the nature of Christian discipleship, and of life in contemporary society. In fact, preaching done in this mode can continually renew the preacher and the office of preaching itself, because sermons will emerge repeatedly at the point where the Bible intersects faith and life.

Historical Faith and Historical Facts

From time to time in these chapters we have come upon a phenomenon without exploring it, a certain tension between what the Bible says and what appear to have been the facts of the matter. For example, we recognize that some New Testament letters that claim to have been written by Paul were almost certainly written later by someone else in his name. Parallel problems exist with regard to the authorship of most biblical books. Implicit in the Synoptists' handling of the divorce question is the fact that each of them has Jesus say what in fact he probably did not say. Preachers who have been sensitized to the conclusions and working hypotheses of biblical critics are often left uncertain about the effect of these views on the preaching of the Bible at certain points, or else they appear to preach as if they did not know that there was serious doubt about the historical accuracy of the text. The renewal of biblical preaching requires that such matters be faced, even if they cannot be dealt with comprehensively in this context. We shall restrict ourselves to three aspects of the matter—the difference between the task of exegesis and historical reconstruction, various responses to the discrepancy in the results of both, and the special question of the historical Jesus.

The distinction between the exegetical task and that of historical reconstruction clearly pertains primarily to narratives that purport to be accounts of events; narrative reports of visions, on the other hand, can scarcely be checked historically, and the content of the vision itself is not subject to historical reconstruction at all. At best, one might interpret it psychologically. In the case of narratives in the historical mode, the exegetical task is to understand and present the meaning of the account as it stands. The historical task is to ascertain the relation between the account and what happened, on the one hand, and to reconstruct the event as fully as possible, on the other.

The distinction may come into focus by referring to an example, Jesus' call of the disciples according to Mark 1:16-20. In exegeting the passage, one asks questions like the following: What is the function of this story in the Gospel as a whole? How is the story structured? What is its center of gravity? How does Mark understand Jesus' word, and how does he see the promise to be fulfilled? What is the relation between the command and the promise? Why is the response portrayed the way it is? Why did the oral tradition pare away everything but precisely these elements of the story? (That is, what was the function of telling the story in just this way?) The exegete will find these issues to be illumined by comparing this story with similar reports of how Jesus got his disciples (Mark 2:13-14; Luke 5:1-11; John 1:35-51). In exegeting this story one will not rewrite the text; that is, one will not make it say something it has no interest in. For instance, one will not "explain" that probably these men had talked with Jesus previously, and so make their response more plausible psychologically. Even if that were the case, that is not what the story wants to say. The story has been reduced to those elements which serve religious interests (the authoritative call issued by Jesus) and paradigmatic concerns (the exemplary response of men who leave everything).

When one asks the historical question, How did Jesus acquire his disciples and who were they? one discovers the question is difficult to answer because all the reports have been shaped to serve religious purposes. The historian will also take note of the socioeconomic status of fishermen in Galilee, as well as of publicans, just as he or she will probe the meaning of "Cananaean" in Mark 3:18, and the problems connected with the idea of twelve disciples (see also Luke 22:28-30). Moreover, one will compare the role of the disciples of Jesus with that of the rabbis, and perhaps with that of the guru as well. In other words, the historian gathers clues and evidence from a variety of sources in order to answer the historical questions on the highest level of probability possible.

Although the exegetical task differs from that of historical reconstruction of the event itself, the two tasks affect each other. On the one hand, exegesis of text must precede reconstruction because one must understand the sources before one can use them properly for historical evidence; on the other hand, reconstructing the event shows the extent to which factors other than accurate reporting governed the formation of the text. Where miracle stories are involved, the historical question also includes judgments about what is physically possible and what is psychologically probable.

A full discussion of historiography and its relation to exegesis would expose many other important facets, such as lexicography, the use of analogous materials in antiquity, or the role of archaeological evidence.[4] The purpose here, however, is simply to clarify the fact that the two enterprises are not to be confused. If the distinction is not kept in mind, one can readily assume that in exegeting the text one has at the same time described what happened. If however, the distinction is maintained, one becomes aware that the biblical narratives in the historical mode have been shaped to serve religious and moral ends. They may be deficient in historical information, but they are efficient in expressing the convictions of faith.

The story of Jesus calling the disciples served very well to illustrate the need to distinguish exegesis from historical reconstruction, but precisely because its sparse historical information can be fitted easily with data derived elsewhere it does not illumine the real problem that emerges from distinguishing the two tasks. That problem comes into view when the historical reconstruction of the events diverges markedly from the biblical narrative. For instance it appears that not all twelve tribes participated in the Exodus, that Jericho was already in ruins when Joshua arrived; that Matthew assembled Jesus' sayings into the Sermon on the Mount, and that few of the words attributed to Jesus in John's Gospel were actually said by him. These discrepancies between the facts of the matter and the biblical text are more serious for preaching than the disparity between a book's stated author and the conclusion that actually someone else wrote it in his name. It is precisely these discrepancies that have led many theological students to conclude that biblical criticism is inimical to preaching, just as they have set in motion a whole range of strategies designed to deny that any discrepancy exists or indeed can exist because the Bible is a book that is error-free throughout, in matters of history and science no less than in matters of faith.

The second thing that we need to reflect on is the various possibilities, other than this fundamentalist one, for dealing with the disparity. We may begin by noting several considerations that, while true enough, do not really help. Thus it is inadequate to remind oneself that often the "negative" historical conclusions have turned out to be premature and inadequately based on limited evidence. Likewise it is insufficient simply to read those scholars who raise the fewest questions. Nor is it enough to say that because all historical reconstruction is a matter of degrees of probability, one need not take these reconstructions seriously.

One more adequate way of dealing with the issue is to affirm on theological grounds the necessity of separating historical questions from matters of faith. This view has been developed with numerous nuances especially during the previous generation, but no one has advocated it more convincingly than Bultmann. In this perspective, valid faith is a response solely to the word of God, which in turn is not a historical account whose accuracy one can test by critical means. Rather, the word is an occurrence in which the hearer knows himself addressed and summoned to faith. The occurring of that word is in no way tied to historical facts (other than the fact of Jesus' crucifixion). What matters is that the understanding of human existence before God be expressed adequately. Just as one de-mythologizes a text that speaks of the last judgment in order to expose what is really said about human existence in faith, so one can use inaccurate narratives, such as mira-cle stories or legends, to proclaim the gospel's promise of authentic existence. Many who do not follow Bultmann's use of existentialist categories nonetheless maintain that because the narrative expresses faith's understanding, that understanding can be affirmed and preached whether or not the narrative comports with historical factuality.

The strength of this stance is clear. First of all, it gives free rein to historical inquiry and historical reconstruction; the chips can fall where they may. The historical task is not hampered by the need to make its results preachable. Moreover, the preachableness of the text is not dependent on the historian's conclusions, and it remains clear throughout that faith is response to God's word, not assent to the meaning ascribed to probable history. One can preach boldly from the birth stories even if one is per-suaded that those critics are right who conclude that Jesus was probably born in Nazareth, that the story of the wise men is a legend, and that the silence of Josephus implies that the massacre of the children did not occur. Likewise the non-genuine sayings of Jesus are as serviceable for preaching as are the *ipsissima verba* (at least in principle); whether in fact they are depends on whether the religious meaning they express is as true to the gospel as the words of Jesus himself. In other words, separating the religious meaning of the text from its historical accuracy means that one can be indifferent to the fallout of historical reconstruc-tion because for the purposes of preaching nothing is at stake anyway. Moreover, this approach rehabilitates, in principle, the whole Bible as preachable material, and rescues the preacher from thinking that only that can be preached which has passed muster in the historian's inspection.

There is a great deal to be said for such a stance. Doubtless many preachers could attest to the liberation and empowerment that they experience through it. Moreover, it comports well with form critical exegesis, in which the first questions are not, Did this happen and Did it happen the way it was reported? but rather, Why was this story told? How did it serve the religious faith and moral life of those who transmitted it? Preaching the religious meaning of the story also helps to link today's church to that of the first century whenever the same way of telling a story is shared by both.

The long-range danger, however, is that the Christian faith may lose both its historical rootage and its capacity to interpret its own experience in theological/biblical terms. It is one thing not to be immobilized by historical reconstruction; it is another to become permanently indifferent to it because one believes the Christian faith is wholly independent of what really happened. One cannot think one way about facts and meaning when the Bible is in view, and another way when our own meaning and experience are involved. Indifference to the relation between historical fact and the biblical report can lead all too easily to the view that also today one can believe anything irrespective of our own history, so long as that belief is "meaningful" or "useful." On this basis, it is hard to see what would prevent the Christian faith from becoming an autonomous set of ideas. If in principle it does not matter whether anything reported happened or not so long as the reports themselves are meaningful, then Christianity has changed fundamentally, including its way of thinking—historically. In other words, the stance epitomized by Bultmann—but not simply equatable with him—is invaluable as a critical move in the face of an orthodox defense of the accuracy of all biblical narratives and in the face of the view that only what is historically verifiable can be preached. But as a long-range basis for a constructive theological position to guide the church it becomes deficient.

Another way of dealing with the disparity between report and historical reconstruction (not simply equatable with "bare facts") is to affirm the critical role of historical reconstruction. In other words, one uses the reconstruction in order to clarify and assess what is going on in a particular report or of the event or saying. Moreover, the historical reconstruction can have this function with regard to both the early church and today's church. The force of this becomes more apparent when we remember that the New Testament is but part of what the early church circulated about Jesus and the apostles, and that methodologically the same criteria are brought to bear on canonical as on noncanonical material.

An example may make these formal statements more concrete. Among the sayings-traditions attributed to Jesus, Bultmann isolated a distinctive form, those sayings which formulate the purpose of Jesus, as "I have come to . . . " or a variant of this form, as the following examples show:

1. "Think not that I have come to abolish the law and prophets; I have come not to abolish them but to fulfil them" (Matt. 5:17).
2. "I came not to call the righteous, but sinners" (Mark 2:17).
3. "For I came down from heaven, not to do my own will, but the will of him who sent me" (John 6:38).

4. I have come to destroy sacrifices (Gospel of the Ebionites).
5. I have to destroy the works of the female (Gospel according to the Egyptians).

Bultmann has also concluded, probably rightly, that all these formulations were created by the church, and that none of them was coined by Jesus himself.[5] No. 1 probably came to Matthew from Jewish Christianity; in its present context it introduces a set of sayings that reject the teaching of some Christians that the law had been annulled by Jesus. No. 2 is formulated to interpret the preceding saying, which is a proverb, "Those who are well have no need of a physician, but those who are sick," which was Jesus' justification for consorting with publicans and sinners. No. 3 articulates the Johannine Christology; descending from heaven says in spatial terms what the more abstract formulation in John 1:14 asserts: the Word became flesh. No. 4 expresses the peculiar view of the Ebionites, a group of Jewish Christians known to us from the second century onward. No. 5 expresses the Christian gnostic view, according to which the female principle is that of matter, flesh, and evil world. In other words, each of these formulations can be related to the horizons of those who created and transmitted them. (Being in the canon does not mean that Nos. 1-3 are genuine whereas 4 and 5 are not.)

At this point the historical reconstruction of Jesus allows us to go further. We can now ask, To what extent do these formulations do justice to Jesus insofar as we are able to recover historically who he was and what he was about? It is clear that Nos. 1-3 are in fact legitimated by the historical Jesus, but not Nos. 4-5. In other words, the former group is true to Jesus, whereas the latter two are not. This means that the Christians who created Nos. 1-3 and who transmitted them and hence accepted them did not distort Jesus. Moreover, No. 1 served to check an opposite reading of Jesus in Matthew's church. In the present context No. 2 reminds Mark's church that it too must go to sinners and outcasts. The context of No. 3 makes it clear that its function is to guard against tendencies on the part of some in the Johannine church to exclude others. In other words, Nos. 1-3 serve to check trends within the church, whereas Nos. 4-5 simply legitimate the point of view of particular types of Christianity; Nos. 1-3 have a prophetic function, Nos. 4-5 an ideological one. Considerations such as these show what is meant by saying that historical reconstruction (in the case of Jesus, the negative conclusion about genuineness of all of these sayings) can help us assess what is going on in the first-and second-century church.

Precisely the same holds true with regard to the contemporary church, as the following examples show:

Jesus came to teach us how to live.
Jesus came to liberate his people from oppressive Roman power.
Jesus came to teach nonviolent love.
Jesus came to free us from legalism.
Jesus came to share his faith with others.
Jesus came to show us what God is like.

On a given Sunday all of these sayings, and more, are said concurrently by the church. Are they all equally valid because each of them is meaningful to a group? Do any of them accord with the purpose of Jesus, insofar as this can be reconstructed historically? In other words, historical reconstruction, probable and ever shifting though it be, can play an important critical role in assessing things said about Jesus today.

Finally, the question of the relation between historical reconstruction and biblical narratives (and the Christian faith that permeates them) comes to a peculiar head in relation to the historical Jesus as a whole. Does the Jesus who emerges from careful historical analysis and reconstruction play any role in preaching? Or, as Bultmann insisted, is this historically ascertained Jesus of no significance at all for preaching? Elsewhere I have written at length on this problem.[6] Here it must suffice to make several observations in support of the view that one can indeed preach this historical Jesus without forfeiting faith itself.

One reason Bultmann opposed preaching the historical Jesus—the Jesus reconstructed by a critical historiography—is that he believed that doing so was a subtle way of making faith easier, of "legitmating" the gospel by providing historical proof for its claims. Actually, however, the historical Jesus does not eliminate the need for a decision of faith, a decision for or against Jesus. Rather, because no historical event or person is self-validating but always inherently ambiguous, the historical Jesus who then called for a decision still calls for a response from those who encounter the reconstruction. For example, his words, "Blessed are the poor in spirit, for yours is the kingdom of heaven," or "Not what goes into the mouth defiles a man, but what comes out of the mouth," are not self-evidently valid. Whether one begins living on this basis is not decided by the fact that it was Jesus who said these things; that holds true only for the person who already has faith or who is already committed to Jesus. Anyone can acknowledge that Jesus said these things, but only the person who decides that Jesus was right becomes a Christian, and that decision is what coming to faith is all about. In short, the historical Jesus functions first of all as an event that calls for a response, as an event that becomes a question: Was he right? Is he a valid index of what it means to live rightly before God and among other people? The historical Jesus, in other words, can be preached as a catalytic question, as one who sets in motion reflection about the deepest questions of life before God and who calls for a response. (Manifestly, what was said of the *diatribē* in chapter 2 applies especially to the Jesus material.) What is decisive in our post-Christendom situation is the fact that the historical Jesus can elicit this questioning precisely where the church's Christ wouldn't even get a hearing. The beautiful book by the Marxist Milan Machoveč illustrates this impressively.[7]

Moreover, the historical Jesus—the Jesus recovered by historical work, not some sort of brute fact prior to any interpretation—has a critical function in the life of the church, as already implied by our discussion of the "I have come . . ." sayings. To be sure, it has become clear not only that every reconstruction of Jesus builds into it the values and biases of the historian, but also that the critical method itself is not wholly "value free." Nonetheless, because historiography proceeds on the basis of public evidence and warrants openly discussed and not on the basis of what is "meaningful to me (or us)," it remains the best way of answering the question, Who was Jesus? in such a way that the content of the name "Jesus" is not reduced to what anybody wants it to be. In other words, the historical Jesus confronts the church and its image of Jesus critically, in a way that is parallel to what has been affirmed about the role of tradition in the Bible itself. The Evangelists of course did not present the historical Jesus in distinction from the church's traditions about Jesus—for the simple reason that the distinction never occurred to them and that a historically ascertained (in our sense) Jesus was not available to them even if it had. That, however, does not prevent our using the results of historiography constructively (as a catalytic question) and critically (as a check against the tendency to make Jesus over in our own image).

The third thing to be said here is that the historical Jesus can be preached as a parable. How does one preach a parable? Not the way that is common—to explain it item by item, draw morals from it or allegorize the life out of it. A parable wants not to be explained but to be understood; what it seeks is a response, not the enlightenment of ideas—just as a joke does. What, then, does the nature and function of a parable suggest about the way one might preach the historical Jesus? Several observations come to mind.

(a) A parable is a rudimentary story, a cartoon in which only the essentials of the plot are used. So in preaching Jesus, one tells a rudimentary story. There is much about Jesus that we do not and cannot know historically; yet the shape of the plot is clear enough to tell, and it is that plot which matters.

(b) A parable is not an illustration of a general truth; illustrations are brought into relation to a truth or idea that can be understood independently. That is inherent in the nature of illustrations, as every preacher knows. But a parable is not an illustration. In parables, the full meaning depends precisely on the parable, on its plot and characters. Change the plot, and the meaning changes. If the parable of the good Samaritan reported that a pious Jew cared for that victim of crime in the streets, then the whole meaning would be different. In parables, there is a subtle relation between the story and meaning because the story does not illustrate something external to itself but embodies its meaning in the plot itself. Likewise, the story of Jesus is parable-like because it does not illustrate an idea external to itself; rather the truth depends on the story. To be sure, one can use Jesus as an illustration. But then it is not Jesus who is being preached, but that other thing which he is brought in to illustrate. In such sermons, Jesus actually illustrates a moral truth, and so becomes an example. Consequently, it is not surprising that using Jesus as an illustration and moralizing usually go hand in hand.

(c) Parables do not explain but challenge and expose. They challenge the hearer and expose him or her through the response that is evoked. Here, too, the parable is like a joke. If I do not laugh at a joke, I manifest something about myself, perhaps that I do not "get it" or have no sense of humor or do not enjoy that kind of story. So too, how I respond to a parable shows who I am. The Jesus-story has the capacity to reveal something about the hearer; how one responds to the story of that life manifests who we are and whom we trust. If we respond by thinking that he was rather naïve, we show that we regard ourselves as knowing better, as being more sophisticated. If we say he was wrong, we show that we believe that we are right. If we say that he was right, we obligate ourselves to realign our lives accordingly. Because the historical Jesus is neither self-explanatory nor self-validating, he calls for a decision just as the parable evokes a response. Just as the meaning of the parable is not self-evident, so the validity of Jesus is neither self-evident nor provable. In both cases, those who "get it" must (may!) change. It was that way then in Galilee; it is that way now. Because the plot, the configuration, of the event called Jesus has the capacity to evoke the response of the self to a self, one can indeed preach the historical Jesus. It can be done in a way that is profoundly biblical.

In Retrospect

The foregoing chapters have emphasized the constructive possibilities for preaching that are latent in a thoroughly historical understanding of the thorougly historical Bible. Accordingly, it accented the ways in which the Bible, at every stage of its development, was embedded in the histories of Israel and of the church. The intent was not negative—to deprive the Bible of its authority by showing how thoroughly contingent it is upon historical circumstances. Rather, the intent was positive—to suggest that the Bible comes into its own when its contingency is affirmed unhesitatingly. Put in more traditional language, we have pressed the particularity of the biblical revelation. In retrospect, several concluding comments appear to be appropriate.

First, what has been said here assumed that the Bible is preached in the context of Christian worship. This setting itself provides an interpretive matrix in which the congregation hears, reads, celebrates, sings its Scripture. The congregation's experience of Scripture is not limited to the sermon. Another book needs to be written that explores the interaction between the total worship experience and biblical preaching as developed in this discussion. Such a book would explore the role of the Bible in providing root metaphors as well as a narrative framework by which Christians can understand reality, and in turn experience it. It would also discuss the ways in which the Bible's own understanding of worship exercises a critique of much that passes for "meaningful worship" today. In other words, such a book would extend the dialectical role of the Bible in the church to the particular situation of worship, showing how the Bible both nourishes and criticizes the church's worship.

Second, the emphasis on historical study, as well as the brief discussion of the historical Jesus, should not be construed to mean that only what survived the historian's fire is preachable (*e.g.*, only what Jesus really said, only if Paul actually wrote Colossians, or if "it really happened"). That would be silly. It would also subvert the whole intent of the book. Instead of helping historical criticism to put the Bible back into the hands of the preacher, it would in effect deprive the preacher of the historically studied Bible indefinitely. To be sure, historical understanding includes judgments about historical accuracy of what is stated. But it includes a great deal more, especially the functions of the material in the life of the communities of faith. The purpose of biblical criticism is not simply to ascertain "the facts" but to understand the text. One engages in historical criticism not in order to ascertain whether a text is factually accurate enough to be preachable, but in order to understand what the text was saying and doing when it came into existence. Other types of biblical study can enrich historical understanding, but they cannot substitute for it. This is because historical understanding links the particularities of "what it meant" with "what it means."

Third, the emphasis on the historical approach also assumed that historical study alone does not generate the conviction that the Bible is profoundly and disturbingly right. That is, historical study does not establish, let alone prove, the religious and moral authority of the Bible. Actually, no method as such can do that. Nor can a robust and fearless use of historical criticism yield the moral passion necessary for effective preaching. These convictions and commitments are indeed often nourished and focused as a result of historical understanding, but inherently they derive from the capacity of the biblical insight to persuade the reader who takes the Bible seriously.

Fourth, the particularities and internal diversity of the Bible which historical criticism exposes call for a theological framework in which both the various particularities and the overall character of such a Bible have an appropriate place. That theological framework too is not acquired by exegeting one more biblical passage, though it may be clarified by exegesis. Rather, it emerges in the process of ascertaining what the Christian faith is all about, and how it continually intersects with human life. In short, the preacher should be a journeyman theologian in order to preach from the Bible. The view of biblical preaching advocated here implies not only that the preacher will be a serious exegete but also a serious theologian—one who ponders and probes rudimentary affirmations of the Christian faith in light of human life until they become clear and convincing.

Finally, this book has been written in the conviction that people are hungry for preaching that is biblical, for a word that illumines life and creates an opening for a liberating alternative with discipline. It was also written in the conviction that preaching is a vital aspect of the Christian ministry, and that no alternative form of communication, be it ever so effective, can substitute for an articulate word in the long run. True, people are hungry not only for sound preaching, nor can preaching alone renew the church. Only the gospel can do that. Still, because biblical preaching is the decisive way of releasing the gospel, biblical preaching must be renewed. And it can be.

Chapter Five

To Be Specific: Three Sermons

It is with a generous amount of fear and trembling that the following sermons are included. To bend a line from Amos of Tekoa, "I am neither a homiletician, nor the son of a homiletician." However, the sermons are presented not as homiletical models, but as specific instances when I have sought to bear witness to the word that I heard in the texts. Despite the diversity of these sermons, they all suggest (I trust) what I mean by taking the Bible seriously in preaching.

Each of the sermons has been preached. Only slight editorial changes have been made to facilitate reading. These particular sermons have been selected because they make concrete certain motifs that have appeared in the foregoing chapters. To make the connection clear, notations have been provided at certain points.

None of the sermons is offered as a model to be imitated. No sermon, mine or anyone else's, will embody everything that this book has discussed and advocated. To produce a sermon that achieved that would be to develop a sermon on the basis of a stencil. If sharing these instances in which I have struggled to let the text come through into today's situation will help preachers do the same, then including them will have achieved its aim.

I
Suppose We Count on God's Goodness

Love of footnotes is probably the occupational hazard of a professor, even in the pulpit. I have often wished there

This sermon was preached at Mercer University, November 1, 1974, and at University worship, Emory University, November 16, 1975.

were a way of including footnotes in a sermon. So today I want to put a footnote first, some reflections on being a preacher of parables.[1]

Whenever I teach or preach the parables of Jesus, I feel more uneasy than with other kinds of texts. This uneasiness comes from the fear that by interpreting the parable I have got everything backwards, because a parable is not a story which *we* interpret, even less a story seeking an explanation. A parable is not something that needs my interpretation, a passive object which receives the benefit of my insight. Rather, a parable is a story that interprets me. It uncovers truth about the hearer and reader. That is why the parables of Jesus have disclosure power. What the parables ask for is not interpretation but understanding and appropriation. The right response to a parable is, "Man, that's the way it is!" When the parable comes through to us, something of Jesus reaches us. And when that happens, we find ourselves at crossroads where fundamental decisions are made. My task is not to *explain* the parable, but to help it on its way to our conscience. The job of the preacher of the parables is to keep from intruding between you and the story.

Sometimes, however, it is necessary to intervene between the story and the hearer in order to help the hearing along. Sometimes this involves removing obstacles to hearing. Sometimes it involves making sure that we are hearing right accents. Sometimes, as in a museum of modern art, it means insisting that we linger long enough and do not turn away too soon because we don't like it. This is especially important when we hear the parable of the day. Listen carefully, if you will, to the parable of the hired help.

For the kingdom of heaven is like a householder who went out early in the morning to hire laborers for his vineyard.

After agreeing with the laborers for a denarius a day, he sent them into his vineyard. And going out about the third hour he saw others standing idle in the market place; and to them he said, "You go into the vineyard too, and whatever is right I will give you." So they went. Going out again about the sixth hour and the ninth hour, he did the same. And about the eleventh hour he went out and found others standing; and he said to them, "Why do you stand here idle all day?" They said to him, "Because no one has hired us." He said to them, "You go into the vineyard too." And when evening came, the owner of the vineyard said to his steward, "Call the laborers and pay them their wages, beginning with the last, up to the first." And when those hired about the eleventh hour came, each of them received a denarius. Now when the first came, they thought they would receive more; but each of them also received a denarius. And on receiving it they grumbled at the householder, saying, "These last worked only one hour, and you have made them equal to us who have borne the burden of the day and the scorching heat." But he replied to one of them, "Friend, I am doing you no wrong; did you not agree with me for a denarius? Take what belongs to you, and go; I choose to give to this last as I give to you. Am I not allowed to do what I choose with what belongs to me? Or do you begrudge my generosity?" So the last will be first, and first last. (Matt. 20:1-16)

We are plainly offended by this story.[2] The more sensitive we become to the demands of justice and equity, the more offended we become. It runs counter to our instinct for what is fair. Intuitively we identify with the workers who lodge a double complaint: "We worked all day and the others only a few hours; besides, we had to work when it was hot and they worked after it cooled off." That everyone should get the same pay regardless of the time or conditions is simply outrageous. The fact that the farmer kept his word and paid those who worked all day exactly what he said he would gets lost because he paid the rest the same amount.

We are also offended by the fact that it was Jesus who told

the story. What's a nice guy like Jesus doing telling a story like this? Isn't Jesus supposed to be revealing God to man? Does he really mean to suggest that God is as unfair as this farmer? We can admire Jesus for telling the story of the good Samaritan because even if that story puts the bite on us to be neighbors, we can get with that story. But this story makes us wonder what Jesus was up to in telling it in the first place. We can applaud him for telling stories that deliberately irritated his critics in the religious establishment, but why would he tell a story that offends the moral sensitivities of persons like us who are on his side?

We assume of course that we ought not be offended. We take it for granted that while the story might imply criticism of us, it surely would not run counter to our deepest instincts of fairness. And so we get rid of the offense by saying that if only we interpreted the story correctly, we would be able to agree with it, and then we would agree with Jesus too. There must be a deeper meaning, one congenial to our sensibilities. For example, one interpreter suggested that Jesus used the story to say that every man deserves a living wage. Some of us can get with that right away, for now Jesus is advocating a guaranteed annual income. He was so far ahead of his time that in his own way he taught "From each according to his ability, to each according to his need." Once we interpret the story in this way, we find that we no longer identify with the grumblers but with the farmer because he is so farsighted. After making this interpretative move, we need only urge one another to work harder for a more equitable distribution of wealth, and pronounce the benediction, because our own alienation from the Protestant work ethic has been confirmed by Jesus himself.

There are two things wrong with this. One has to do with the story, the other with ourselves. As far as the story is concerned, this congenial interpretation does not really follow the plot, and especially the punch line of the story does not seem to fit. If the congenial interpretation were on target, we would expect the farmer to say something like, "Don't you realize that everyone needs at least a minimum to live on?" But the story has the farmer speak of his goodness. Somehow the point has to do with his goodness, not the needs of the poor workers. Moreover, the story carefully points out that those who worked only one hour were paid first and got their money in the presence of the others. Surely the reaction of those who worked all day was no surprise. In fact it is essential to the story. This farmer *intends* to offend those who worked longest, and underlines this by accusing them of being irritated at his goodness. If we are faithful to the story, we must keep our eye on the contrast between goodness and fairness.[3]

The congenial social interpretation also runs afoul of ourselves because it quickly removes the offense and encourages us to identify with the farmer. But it is at least equally possible that Jesus meant for us to be shocked. As a matter of fact, many of Jesus' parables have this shock value built into them. That is how he cuts through our prevailing assumptions and holds up a mirror to ourselves.

Our story illumines who we are by the way it exposes our sympathies. The way we relate to those who worked most and to those who worked least shows us the truth about ourselves.

Most of us identify with those who worked longest not simply because we think *they* got a raw deal but because we think *we* get one too. Like the day-long workers in the story, even though we get exactly what we bargained for, we begin to feel gypped when we see someone do better. The farmer pointed out, you recall, that he was not unfair to them, because he paid them exactly what he said he would.

It is the sight of others, who worked less for the same reward, that first makes us feel cheated, then feel sorry for ourselves. The fairness we demand is not in terms of our commitments but in terms of what our neighbor gets. What student has not complained because his roommate got the same grade for but half the work, irrespective of the quality? We are unable to congratulate her for getting the same grade for but half the effort because we believe that the reward must be scaled to effort.

Our identity is based on those rewards which we can compare, whether grades, positions, or salary. Our sense of self-worth is all wrapped up in competitive effort and reward. Therefore we interpret reality by this schema; indeed, the ultimate reality of God is expected to conform to it as well. In fact, God is the guarantor of this system. And so we do not measure the fairness of God by whether he keeps his word but by comparing what *we* receive with what our neighbors get.

Moreover, the demand for fairness can be an expression of self-delusion. We sometimes demand fairness because we believe that we deserve more. I never heard of anyone demanding fairness who did not think that if he got it he would gain. Somehow it does not occur to us that fairness might bring us less than we have, that a truly rigorous and impartial justice will find us on the short end of the stick. We assume that if God is good, he will be fair, and if he is fair we will come out ahead because we deserve more. And here is where we are in danger of self-deception about our goodness.

The same mentality appears in the form of its opposite—a neurotic feeling of self-contempt, a sick belief that God's fairness will bring about our misery because we have been so bad, and are worth so little. Such a person has a masochistic theology, always expecting the worst as punishment. But for most of us, the self-deception does not take the form of undervaluation but of overvaluation. And so we identify with those who believe they deserve more than others.

On the other hand, few of us identify with those who were hired near quitting time and got paid more than they earned. These are the men who expected fairness but benefitted from goodness, from a sheer generosity that ignored achievement. Yet in countless ways, big and small, this is who we are. If life were totally a matter of strict fairness, it would scarcely be tolerable. Who wants to receive back from others—our roommates, husbands or wives, parents or siblings—exactly what we gave them? Is not life made tolerable, and sometimes joyous, by the fact that those closest to us overlook our tart words, ignore what is said in times of fatigue and bad moods, set aside the deeds that hurt? Is this not what love and compassion are all about? Why, then, do we not see ourselves among those who worked least?

We resist identifying with those who benefit from goodness because we hate to acknowledge that we did not deserve the goodness we ourselves received. We tell ourselves that we deserve even our good fortune. "It couldn't have happened to a nicer guy." The idea that in the mystery of things we get better than we deserve is too disturbing to our way of valuing ourselves. Once we live by tit for tat, we resist the possibility that we benefit from another kind of system, that we receive better than we give, that what makes life humane is the repeated experience of undeserved goodness, that life actually exists by the grace of God. Instead of allowing these experiences of undeserved goodness to call into question our allegiances to the system of fairness, we pull these experiences into the reward system and tell ourselves that in the last analysis we deserved them. The offense of goodness is total, for it calls into question that network of assumptions and trusts by which we live.

No wonder we are offended by our story, and no wonder we welcome any interpretation that does not challenge us so deeply. No wonder we wish Jesus had never told the story, or that those who heard it would have fogotten it. That they did not forget it shows that it must have haunted them, hectored their self-assurance until it redeemed them from illusion and thrust them into the mind-blowing freedom of life by God's grace. Wherever that happens, it becomes clear that the parable has done its work, and that it could not do this without offense, anymore than the man who told it could fulfill his commission without telling such a story. For the story is about the kingdom of God, as is the story of Jesus himself.

The punch line is the key: to those who grumbled, the farmer said, "Do you begrudge my goodness?" That is, "Do you begrudge the goodness of God made manifest in the way his kingdom comes?" There was an edge to the question because repeatedly people were offended by Jesus at this very point.[4] Imagine this man announcing to those who, in the eyes of the deserving, deserved nothing, "To you belongs the kingdom of God." Imagine actually taking the beachhead of the kingdom to those five o'clock folk who deserved almost nothing—the poor, the outcast, the despised extortioners and collectors of taxes for Rome. But when God comes through as God, these will know that it is not fairness but goodness that overwhelms them.

Suppose we believed in the goodness of God! Suppose this parable had the power to bug us until we began to move away from demanding God's fairness and toward celebrating his goodness. What difference would it make if we believed that God's goodness was not metered out on the basis of fairness but of love?[5]

First, we would understand that God is for us, whether we win, lose, or draw, and that he is for us because he wants to be, not because we maneuver him into paying us off. We would see that our relation to the ultimate reality does not depend on our goodness but on his; and that the manifestation of his goodness occurs freely and not on the merit system. Once we see this, we are emancipated from the compulsion to understand God as the great paymaster.

Second, we are liberated from the delusions with which we understand whatever goodness we do have. We are free to see it for what it is. Now we need no longer insist on how much we deserve because we can see that our goodness is such a mixed bag. Much of it comes from all sorts of motives and impulses; a good deal of it is the result of other people's influence on us, more of a gift than an accomplishment of our own. Once we stop demanding that we be rewarded fairly, we are free to see ourselves accurately for the first time, and not fear that the truth will destroy us. We can accept our failure, our weakness and vulnerability because we know we do not have to be successful in order to keep God positively disposed toward us. Misfortune and failure are no longer signs of God's hostility because good fortune and success are not the signs of his love based on reward.

Third, if we trusted the free goodness of God, we would be free to relate to our neighbors in a new way. We would not keep the system of rewards going by telling those less fortunate than we that they are in the mess they are in because they deserve to be. If they would only work harder, do better, be more like us, they would not be on welfare. We would also be free from jealousy of those more fortunate, because the good fortune of others would not threaten our identity and sense of worth. Then we would be free to rejoice with those who rejoice, as Paul puts it, because our relative fortunes would no longer be an index of what either of us deserves. If we believed in the goodness of God, we would accept the fact that he sends the sunshine and rain on good and bad alike, and we would cease thinking that the sinners deserve either a drought or a flood.

What I am trying to say is that if we followed the grain of our story, if we believed in the goodness of God rather than insisted on his fairness, we would be liberated at the center of life to live by the grace of God, to accept life as it comes, the good with the bad. Many experiences will tell us nothing about what we deserve, for we all live by the goodness and grace of God who gives us more than we earn.

In conclusion, let me read the story again, this time in a paraphrase written by a young man in jail who discovered what it's all about.

The time came for the trucks and boats to get loaded down at the flour mill. They needs a lot more guys to put the sacks on the trucks and boats and on freight cars. So the foreman on the first shift goes up to the union hall where guys were hangin' around waitin' for a job to come along so they can make a few bucks.

The foreman makes a deal with a bunch of guys to load a big trailer truck. He said he's gonna pay them $1.25 an hour to work on his shift. So they came to work at six A.M. and worked hard loading up the truck.

About nine o'clock some other guys come around looking for a job, and the foreman says, "OK, you're on, get to work," but he don't tell them what he would pay. He just says, "I'll make it right with ya." So they started to work. About noon some of the winos that had been sleeping under the old buildings got sobered and came looking for a job to get more money so they can get stoned that night, and they asked for a job. They got one, and the foreman says, "I'll make it right with ya," and they starts to work, but not very hard 'cause they are still a little sick from getting stoned the night before.

To Be Specific: Three Sermons

They is still a lot of flour to put on the trucks, so when some big kids that goes to high school comes by after school he gives them a job and says, "I'll make it right with ya." And they likes to show everybody what big guys they is and how strong their muscles is, so they works hard and gets all sweaty. The foreman puts on some more guys just when his shift is most over and they only work for an hour. Then everything was loaded and the truck pulls out, the freight cars get their doors closed and the engine comes and pulls them away, and the boats start to send out a lots of smoke and blow their whistles like hell, and the little tugs come and the big boats goes away, too.

Now comes the time when everybody gets paid off. They get in a line and everybody is pushin' 'cause they wants to get paid first. The foreman has got their money in little envelopes to give them. Everybody is happy. The guys that was at the union hall thinks about the food they can buy, the winos is thinkin' about the wine and beer they gonna get, and the high school kids about a new pair of pants and stuff like that.

When the foreman gives out the money, everybody is got the same money—the ones from the union hall that worked all day, the winos, the high schools kids, and the ones that got a job near the end of the day. This makes everybody mad except the ones that don't work so hard; but mostly the ones who worked all day started to yell and say that they was gonna start a strike, and carry signs sayin' UNFAIR.

The foreman says, "Now wait a minute, you guys—I kept my deal with all of you guys—ya got no kick comin', see! I told the first ones $1.25 an hour, that's what I paid you, right?" And they said, "That's right." Then the foreman says, "I told the rest of you guys that I'd make it right with ya and I did pretty good by ya, didn't I?" And they said he did. "I kept my deal and I didn't do nothin' wrong, and you got no kick comin'. That's the way I wanta do it, and that's the way it's gonna be. I just wants to give the high school kids a break and help them out 'cause I like them. What's wrong with that?" The first guys couldn't think of anything except they still thinks that they are getting cheated. But they figures that the foreman kept his word and did what he was supposed to with the deal he made, and that's fair enough, but they didn't like it.

This story tells us that God can treat us the way he does

cause of his love and not on account of how much stuff we do. Course this don't mean that you can go snatchin' purses and robbin' parkin' meters, and shop liftin'. But it does mean that God treats you good and keeps his deals too.[6]

II

Jesus and Contemporary Heresy

Good Friday is not a day for preaching so much as it is a day for reflection. By reflection I do not mean introspection, a devout fascination with the contours of our navels; nor do I mean pious musing about the agonies of Jesus. Rather, I have in mind a sober and unromantic mulling over of the import of that sequence of events which we know as the Passion story.

The Passion story is not the story which the history detectives piece together by carefully sifting the accounts in order to get at the facts, which are then used to reconstruct what really happened. That is an important undertaking, but its result is not the Passion story. By Passion story we mean a narrative of Jesus' last days, told in such a way as to expose the interplay of religious issues. In the Passion story, event and interpretation are fused so that the meaning is built into the dynamic of the story and is not merely attached like a moral.

This is why the story of the trial and execution of Jesus continues to be one of those narratives which captures our imagination. It evokes pathos, moral outrage, and compassion; it is one of those stories which has never been fully understood, and even less has it been explained completely. In the history of Christian theology, several major interpretations have been developed, and we call them "theories of the atonement." Yet it is not theories that

This sermon was preached at Mercer University, 1973.

captivate us but the narrative and the man. The New Testament itself contains more than one way of presenting the Passion story. I invite you to reflect with me on John's way of telling the story.[1]

John's account is even more stylized than the others. His narrative does not have the story of Jesus in Gethsemane, where Jesus went through a struggle over the prospect of death. John's Jesus is too sovereign in every situation to have any second thoughts. Nor does John call attention to Jesus' suffering on the cross. It is not the humanness of Jesus that interests him but his imperturbable mastery of the situation. For John regards the whole event of Jesus as the decisive disclosure of God and humanity, and he tells the Passion story accordingly. It is like a one-act drama which uses a particular situation to expose fundamental aspects of the human situation as a whole.

At this point, I must say a word about the historical accuracy of our story. I said our story was stylized. That is, what John is showing us by means of Pilate and the priests is the character of the world, the character of humanity when it prefers darkness to light.[2] Because these protagonists in the story represent the world, they represent *us*. John is not chiefly interested in showing us how they acted, but how we act. It's often said that Christians exonerated Pilate so as to make the church look good in Roman eyes. But Pilate is not really exonerated but portrayed as ludicrous. Pilate is not made a hero because John feared the Roman cops; rather he is made into a comic figure because John did not fear them. It is the inner basis of this freedom with regard to Pilate that is the secret of our story. Our story does not give us an accurate portrayal of Pilate. It is contradicted by everything we know about this scoundrel. Nor does our story give us an accurate portrayal of the Jewish leaders and their motives. That John's Gospel as a whole has played a major role in Christian anti-Semitism is a sad fact which we must not overlook, especially on Good Friday—the day when repeatedly Jews have sat in dread.

What interests me this morning is the dynamic of the three characters: the religious establishment, the embodiment of political power, and Jesus. The religious establishment is portrayed as disturbed by the impact Jesus is making. Seven chapters earlier, John had told the story of the resuscitated Lazarus, and this event was reported to the Pharisees. They convened the council and John formulates the problem they faced: "What are we to do? For this man performs many signs. If we let him go on thus, every one will believe in him, and the Romans will come and destroy both our holy place and our nation." They recognize that the security of the nation rests on the stability of the temple, for the High Priest was the one with whom the Romans negotiated. If the priesthood were undermined by this free lancer from Nazareth, Rome would intervene. What to do? But the High Priest was a wily politician who saw a way out. So he said, "You know nothing at all; you do not understand that it is expedient for you that one man should die for the people, and that the whole nation should not perish." That is, "Let's arrange it so that the Romans will take care of Jesus. By sacrificing this Jesus, we will get rid of him and at the same take the heat off us." As it turned out, they had the cooperation of Judas.

After Jesus was arrested, he was taken to the High Priest for a hearing, and then they took him to Pilate. Now comes the scene that is the focus of our attention. The way John tells the story, Pilate does not want to get involved, but finds himself being manipulated. And before he knows it, he has been forced to cooperate. The story is told with trenchant irony, for while Jesus is condemned to death, the connivers condemn themselves without knowing it. Subtly the roles are reversed: the accused becomes the judge, and the judge and the accusers become guilty. Listen to how the story unfolds:

> Then Pilate took Jesus and scourged him. And the soldiers plaited a crown of thorns, and put it on his head, and arrayed him in a purple robe; they came up to him, saying, "Hail, King of the Jews!" and struck him with their hands. Pilate went out again, and said to them, "See, I am bringing him out to you, that you may know that I find no crime in him." So Jesus came out, wearing the crown of thorns and the purple robe. Pilate said to them, "Behold the man!" When the chief priests and the officers saw him, they cried out, "Crucify him, crucify him!" Pilate said to them, "Take him yourselves and crucify him, for I find no crime in him." The Jews answered him, "We have a law, and by that law he ought to die, because he has made himself the Son of God." When Pilate heard these words, he was the more afraid; he entered the praetorium again and said to Jesus, "Where are you from?" But Jesus gave no answer. Pilate therefore said to him, "You will not speak to me? Do you not know that I have power to release you, and power to crucify you?" Jesus answered him, "You would have no power over me unless it had been given you from above; therefore he who delivered me to you has the greater sin."
>
> Upon this Pilate sought to release him, but the Jews cried out, "If you release this man, you are not Caesar's friend; every one who makes himself a king sets himself against Caesar." When Pilate heard these words, he brought Jesus out and sat down on the judgment seat at a place called The Pavement, and in Hebrew, Gabbatha. Now it was the day of Preparation for the Passover; it was the sixth hour. He said to the Jews, "Behold your King!" They cried out, "Away with him, away with him, crucify him!" Pilate said to them, "Shall I crucify your King?" The chief priests answered, "We have no king but Caesar." Then he handed him over to them to be crucified. (John 19:1-16)[3]

I want to highlight three themes embedded in this narrative. The first concerns Jesus. John writes his whole Gospel to show him to be the one who discloses the truth about God and humans. He has Jesus himself say, "For this I was born, and for this I have come into the world, to bear witness to the truth." The situation does not call for a lecture on truth. Here the truth is uncovered by the way the religious establishment and political power deal with Jesus. Truth is exposed here. It happens again and again; it can happen today. We always give away the truth about ourselves by the way we relate to this man. This is true of any figure, especially a controversial one. Tell me what you think of Billy Graham or Lester Maddox, and I will know something of who you are. Furthermore, when you deal with persons of substance, what is uncovered lies deeper in ourselves. In the case of Jesus, he uncovers what we trust and value most. That is, he uncovers that which is our god. This comes clear as we look at the other characters in the story.

Next, let's look at Pilate. He is portrayed as a man who means well but who is manipulated into doing what he knows is wrong. Even though he does not understand what Jesus is talking about, he knows that this is a frame-up, and that Jesus has not done anything which calls for the death penalty. Yet he ends up sentencing him to death. Where is the Achilles' heel? It is the passion to preserve his position with Caesar. What seals Jesus' fate is the word of the crowd, "If you release this man, you are not Caesar's friend; everyone who makes himself a king sets himself against Caesar." I doubt whether Pilate needed that lecture in political science. But its function was not to instruct his mind but to expose his heart, to find his Achilles' heel. And it worked.

The story of Pilate suggests that the morality of political power is ultimately self-preservation after all.[4] The antics of the White House with regard to the Watergate affair is clear documentation of what our story shows. Pilate comes on as a fair-minded official who ostensibly seeks the truth about the accused. But when the power play begins, he can be maneuvered, for as soon as he must risk something for the truth, he begins to waffle. He might risk his job to intercede for a fellow Roman, for someone who really mattered. But for this provincial who will not even cooperate? So justice for the powerless is eclipsed by self-preservation of the powerful. In a crunch, political power first preserves itself, and sacrifices the vulnerable.

Some of us may be surprised by this; others have known it long ago. The Vietnam debacle should have taken away all illusions about government, since government of whatever administration has told us everything but the truth in order to preserve itself. When government is as cynical about truth as was Pilate, it can be maneuvered into self-contradiction just as it can be manipulated by the cynical. When power without morality is caught between integrity and cynicism, it repeatedly capitulates because it is guided by what it can get by with. Precisely because politics is the art of compromise, of give and take, of sacrificing this in order to gain that, those who depend on government can never be sure when they might be sacrificed for some other purpose—as the poor, the black, the sick, and the disinherited can testify.

One heresy of our time is the assumption that it is otherwise, that political power is fundamentally moral, that it can save us from our sins. Like Pilate, it can say, "I have power to release you and power to execute you," but it does not have freedom to act. Pilate did not realize that he was not free to exercise his power according to his conscience but that he could be manipulated for the sake of law and order. Shall he end up on the side of unrest and disorder simply to protect this man? Surely the life of one innocent man is not too high a price for law and order. And so it is that this uncooperative Jesus unmasks the pretensions of political power, and discloses the heresy of accepting those pretensions.

The third actor I want to reflect on emerges at the climax of our story, namely the religious establishment. When the crowd yells, "Away with him, away with him, crucify him," Pilate fires a last shot: he taunts them with the question, "Shall I crucify your King?" And the chief priests reply, "We have no king but Caesar." This is the ultimate heresy of the day, of that day and of our day. True, in the story this assertion is part of the effort to manipulate Pilate, part of the scheme to get him to do what they want by insisting that they are acting out of loyalty to Caesar. They didn't really mean it. Nonetheless, they say more than they mean to say. They really say the truth without knowing it. This patriotic gesture is really a confession of moral bankruptcy. And it is the confession of a major part of the contemporary American mind. It has had the blessing of the church.

Let us not make the mistake of looking down on these priests. In John's Gospel, things are seldom straightforward historical facts. There is usually more than one level of meaning. What John is showing us is that the defendant unmasks the heresy of religious devotion to the state. In our day, the heresies which are most powerful have to do more with the Father than with the Son. They have to do with the deification of the state, or with the veneration of political power, with the adoration of the state as if it were god, the creator and preserver of all things good.

What is it that gets us up tight most? Not what people think about Jesus but what people think about government. A few years ago, there was a small flap when one of the Beatles said they were more popular than Jesus. But that was nothing compared to the intensity of feeling and anxiety connected with amnesty, or over the right to question the fundamental morality of government. Today, government leaves no area of life untouched; worst of all, it claims the right to decide what is good and what is right, and it sanctifies its judgment with religiosity. In Old Testament times, King Solomon built a chapel in the royal compound; today the chapel has moved into the White House itself. We are induced to acquiesce, to submit to the wisdom of the Pentagon or the White House. We are told, in countless ways, that we do not know enough to make a moral judgment but that government does; we are told that we ought to entrust our whole existence to government because government knows best. In short, we are asked to acquiesce in the unlimited sovereignty of government the way we were once asked to believe in the providence of God.

Wherever the state is invested with such religious aura, there we join the priests and say, "We have no king but Caesar." That is, whenever we acknowledge no allegiance higher than the state we have no criterion for right and wrong by which to judge the state. In a way, this is not surprising, for where God is dead, the state becomes god, for the good of the state becomes the ultimate good to which all other goods are subject. So it is not surprising that for the good of the state, for our honor as we were told, fifty thousand had to die in a futile war. In our silent acquiescence, and in our rejection of those who said no, we shouted our confession, "We have no king but Caesar." And so this defendant in the dock—Jesus—unmasks the supreme heresy of our day.

I am keenly aware that our reflections have been somber, that they have lacked joy and celebration. But after all, this is the day of Jesus' trial and execution. This is the day when his career of uncovering the truth about ourselves comes to a head. And the truth about ourselves is seldom a cause to celebrate, for the truth is that I am not OK nor are you.

Yet precisely in John's Gospel stands the promise which pertains also to what Jesus' trial uncovers about us: "If you continue in my word, you are truly my disciples, and you will know the truth, and the truth will make you free." This Jesus in the dock still has the power to liberate us from illusions and from allegiance to the deified no-god, because he did not cop out but maintained his integrity to the end. According to John his last word was, "It is finished!" and so he became the lamb that takes away the sin of the world—if we let him.

III
Limited Resources, Unlimited Possibilities

At one time or other, all of us have wondered, "Just what am I doing here?" I am not concerned just now with the bewilderment that is a symptom of an unclear vocation. I am concerned now with that gnawing, demoralizing sense of inadequacy which often seeps into the seminary community.

Indeed, the curriculum appears to be designed to rob a student of confidence. On the one hand, horizons are pushed back so that we are overwhelmed by the enormity of the problems we face. The simple pulpit answers for which the church is known are shown to be thin and short. Healing the gnarled and twisted human lives we touch takes far more than "a decision for Christ." Even the task of coming to terms with ourselves turns out to be overwhelming, the more we learn that we cannot run away from who we are and have become at the hands of parents, small-town expectations, or our own illusions. Besides, unsnarling the tangled threads of our society takes more than evangelistic crusades, more than marches, more even than

This sermon was preached at Durham Chapel, Candler School of Theology, Emory University, on January 7, 1975.

hard-won victories in elections. The tension between the remedies for inflation and the remedies for depression stands for the baffling complexity of our world. Our situation is quite like that of the Israelite reconnaisance into Canaan in the time of Moses. You recall that the spies returned not simply with tales on their lips about the milk and honey, but also with terror in their hearts because there were giants in the land—giants so much in command of the situation that there seemed to be no point in pitting the puny resources of the Hebrews against them.

On the other hand, our feeling of adequacy is eroded by the seminary experience itself in another way—we find that we no longer believe what we once believed as firmly as we once believed it. Not only do we become more aware of what the gospel has to contend with, but late one night we might discover that we are no longer sure what the gospel is. All this critical analysis has gotten to us—a pretty good sign that the faculty is doing its job. Even if we learn about the past victories over persecuting caesars, it is not clear that we ourselves could take them on. We are not sure we can use our weapons. True, we have been taught how to disassemble our rifles and to name the parts—you know, J, E, D, P, Q, Proto-Luke and Deutero-Paul. But now we have trouble getting it back together. Some of us are afraid that when we need it most, it will not work for us the way it used to; while others wonder whether there is any firepower at all in such a scripture as the Bible turns out to be.

This deep uneasiness and ambivalence would be more manageable if we could simply concentrate on sorting ourselves out, on finding that most precious commodity of all, identity. The quest for identity has become more important than it ought to be. This is because we are in a bewildered culture, set in the midst of a time and place where people are seeking something to hold onto, something that makes sense, something to count on. For the first time since we Europeans began pushing the Indians back from the shore, it is no longer clear that our children will fare better than we did. For the first time there rises up the spectre of our grandchildren calling us to account for having robbed them by our throw-away economy. It might not be long before my generation will be indicted for believing its own propaganda about the glories of the American way of life, blessed and sanctified by educators, politicians, and clergy. Where is the articulate and incisive person who can tell our people the truth in a way that will be heard? It is fairly easy to be shrill with the truth, but who can say it effectively so that new alternatives appear? Our churches are as uncertain as the culture they bless. What is more disheartening than the Saturday paper, laden with dilemmas and crises on one page, burdened with the church ads on the next—ads which boldly announce sermons and programs which appear to leave our people hungry and groping.

In other words, we are becoming aware of the world and aware of ourselves precisely at a time when we can no longer afford the luxury of finding ourselves above all. The very impulses that brought us here also set our faces toward this hunger for a word of truth or a deed which has integrity. It would be absurd to think that we are the only ones who are caught between massive needs and personal inadequacy, for teachers, social workers, and economists also are in this plight. But my concern is with us.

Our diagnosis has not been thorough, but it is enough to suggest that we need to hear a story. And strangely, it's a story whose point a prosaic mind can miss. In fact, on one level it's completely unbelievable; on another level, it can . . . but why spoil the story in advance?[1]

To Be Specific: Three Sermons

The apostles returned to Jesus, and told him all that they had done and taught. And he said to them, "Come away by yourselves to a lonely place, and rest a while." For many were coming and going, and they had no leisure even to eat. And they went away in the boat to a lonely place by themselves. Now many saw them going, and knew them, and they ran there on foot from all the towns, and got there ahead of them. As he went ashore he saw a great throng, and he had compassion on them, because they were like sheep without a shepherd; and he began to teach them many things. And when it grew late, his disciples came to him and said, "This is a lonely place, and the hour is now late; send them away, to go into the country and villages round about and buy themselves something to eat." But he answered them, "You give them something to eat." And they said to him, "Shall we go and buy two hundred denarii worth of bread, and give it to them to eat?" And he said to them, "How many loaves have you? Go and see." And when they had found out, they said, "Five, and two fish." Then he commanded them all to sit down by companies upon the green grass. So they sat down in groups, by hundreds and by fifties.

And taking the five loaves and the two fish he looked up to heaven, and blessed, and broke the loaves, and gave them to the disciples to set before the people; and he divided the two fish among them all. And they all ate and were satisfied. And they took up twelve baskets full of broken pieces and of the fish. And those who ate the loaves were five thousand men. (Mark 6:30-44)

That story illumines where we find ourselves, and what we may expect. It might not be easy to get with the beat of this story. We have labeled it the story of the Multiplication of the Loaves and Fishes, and tourist guides in the Holy Land will take you to the ruins of a church built on the exact place where it happened. But Mark is not as interested in the miraculous as we are; in fact he doesn't tell us what happened to the bread and fish. He does tell us what happened to people. But back to the story.[2]

Here is a crowd of people, thronging around Jesus. To

him, they suggested sheep without a shepherd, milling about. Have you ever seen shepherdless sheep? We must not think of a dozen sheep fenced in the south 40 of a north Georgia farm. We ought to see bands of sheep in the far West. These herds are wholly dependent on the shepherd for pasture and protection. Take away the shepherd and his dog, and they simply wander around, nibbling their way into danger and death, baa-baaing their fears into the night. Despite our city ways, we have enough imagination left to see that the image is that of our culture with no leadership worth naming, and no truth to feed on. And now it's time to eat.

The disciples were sensitive to the situation and to the needs of persons. They also know where they are—out among the hills and gulleys of Palestine. So they suggest, "This is a lonely place and the hour is now late. Send them away to go into the countryside and villages round about and buy themselves something to eat." What could better combine compassion with realism? They clearly believe in responsible social action based on the contextual ethic.[3]

But Jesus has something else in mind. To such a practical suggestion he responds with something quite ridiculous: "You give them something to eat." The disciples are flabbergasted. So they explode with frustration, "Shall we go and buy 200 denarii worth of bread and give it to them to eat?" That's about eight months' pay. Where are they to get that kind of money just now? No credit card could bail them out.[4]

This is where we find ourselves, is it not? Overwhelmed by need before us and overwhelmed by inadequacy within ourselves, we nonetheless hear this command, "You give them something to eat." And so like our predecessors, we protest that too much is expected of us. "Shall we go somewhere to get supplies?" To paraphrase, Shall we go to

Emory, to graduate school—at least get a D. Min.? Shall we collect supplies from Tillich, or Moltmann, or Reuther? Shall we go to the conservatives, whose churches are growing, or to the charismatics?

But Jesus does not send them anywhere to get supplies. He asks a question so simple and so irrelevant that they wonder whether he is in touch with reality. "How many loaves have you? Go see." What difference does it make how many loaves they had? It wouldn't be enough to feed this crowd. But nonetheless, they go look; perhaps they hope to scrounge up a little anyway. When they return, their report sounds like Mother Hubbard on food stamps: "Sir, we have five loaves and two fish." Things are worse than they thought. That's not even enough for Jesus, and the disciples, not even half a loaf apiece, and those fish weren't twenty-pound salmon either.

Surely Jesus will get back to reality now and dismiss the crowd. There's nothing to be done with such resources. We have no trouble identifying with the disciples. We too stand there with our five sandwiches and two sardines, facing a needy world. It's that old story again: the spies and the giants, David and Goliath, Paul in Ephesus, Schweitzer in Lambaréné, Martin Luther King in Montgomery, you and I in Atlanta. But we cannot ignore the world in order to divide what we have among ourselves, cozy and "fellowshippy" though it would be.

Jesus is not stymied. He orders the crowd to sit in groups of fifties and hundreds. And now he takes those loaves and fish and says the blessing and divides them just as any Jewish father would do at home. Then he gives the bread to the disciples to distribute. Can you imagine their embarrassment as they stood in line, waiting for their turn to get the bread, knowing that ten thousand eyes were watching and five thousand stomachs growling?

Now our curiosity is strained. We want to know how Jesus did it. But curiosity goes hungry while the crowd is fed. Mark wants us to see the people, not the loaves. The crowd had more than enough to eat, and there were twelve baskets of leftovers. And don't ask where they got the baskets either![5]

Mark's picture is coming through now. The crowd is fed when Jesus takes the meager resources and gives his blessing. That's the word of God even for seminarians. Persons can be fed even through our piddling resources. They will be fed not because the loaves and fish belong to us, nor because they are special loaves, but simply because things happen that way when our resources are put at the disposal of Jesus. This would be just as true if we had one loaf and one fish for every man, woman, and child.

If we cannot see this clearly enough on the Synoptic network, we can turn to Paul's: Corinthians, channel 2. The Corinthians do not know what to make of Paul. Paul tells them that they do not understand his role because they do not understand the gospel. They think that the apostle's effectiveness is to be measured by his rhetoric, by his philosophical gyrations, by the power of his ecstatic experiences. When measured by this yardstick, the apostle doesn't come off so well. He has only five loaves and two fish, and there are many sophisticated Corinthians to be fed. They want a preacher about whose prowess they can boast.

Well, says Paul, I can boast too. Listen to his boasting: "Five times I have received at the hands of the Jews the forty lashes less one. Three times I have been beaten with rods; once I was stoned. Three times I have been shipwrecked; a night and a day adrift at sea; on frequent journeys, in danger from rivers, danger from robbers, danger from my own people, danger from Gentiles, danger in the city, danger in the wilderness. . . . And apart from other things, there is the daily pressure upon me of my anxiety for all the churches." What kind of boasting is that? It is boasting about having only five loaves and two fish, or as Paul puts it, "If I must boast, I will boast of the things that show my weakness."

And if this public record has not revealed how weak he is, his private inner life does. So he tells of his religious experience, that element so greatly prized in Corinth—and in Georgia. He was caught up to the third heaven, where he heard wondrous things. Surely this ought to get him beyond the five measly loaves. But now listen as Paul continues: "To keep me from being too elated by the abundance of revelations, a thorn was given me in the flesh, . . . to keep me from being too elated. Three times I besought the Lord about this, that it should leave me; but he said to me, 'My grace is sufficient for you, for my power is made perfect in weakness.' "

There you have it. The same Lord who did not get nervous when he looked down at the little lunch said to Paul, "My power is made perfect in your five loaves." And Paul managed to lay hold of enough grace to say, "I will all the more gladly boast of my weaknesses, that the power of Christ may rest upon me. For the sake of Christ, then, I am content with weaknesses, insults, hardships, persecutions, and calamities; for when I am weak, then I am strong." Paul says this because Christ has blessed him in his weakness, has shown how the power of the gospel is not the same as the strength of the apostle. Mark would have said it this way, "When the disciples have only five loaves and two fish they have plenty because Christ will make it more than enough." I can put it this way: "When I face the world with my limited resources I need not panic because Christ can make them adequate by blessing them."

I recall preaching a sermon so weak that I wished I could have sneaked out the back way. But at the door, a person who seldom commented made it a point to say that the sermon had been helpful. To this day I can't see what it could have been that helped her, but one of my little loaves was blessed and she was fed.

I also recall an incident when I was in the Boston City Hospital taking my clinical training. One day the chaplain called on a patient who had been visited by one of us. The patient said the visit was almost as if God himself had entered his room. The chaplain was eager to find out who made this tremendous call and to read his verbatim report. He found out that the student who made the call didn't bother to write it up because he had no idea that he had been the vehicle for the divine presence, and that his loaf had been blessed enough for a lonely patient to be fed.

All sorts of things happen when our five loaves are put to work. Fifteen years ago, a group of students had only five loaves of determination to be treated equally, and sat in at a lunch counter, and began a revolution. Who knows what you and I might yet be called upon to do or say?[6]

To such a list of experiences you yourself may add—if you risk using your five loaves to feed the crowd. And then this story will come true again, for the point is not what happened to the bread but what happened to the people when the bread was blessed. Generation after generation has been fed by weak disciples serving their own five loaves with Christ's blessing. This is the real apostolic succession, and now it's our turn. You give them something to eat.

Notes

1. On the Malaise of Biblical Preaching

1. The allusion is to Dean M. Kelley, *Why Conservative Churches are Growing* (New York: Harper & Row, 1972).
2. James D. Smart, *The Strange Silence of the Bible in the Church* (Philadelphia: Westminster Press, 1970).
3. Elizabeth Achtemeier, *The Old Testament and the Proclamation of the Gospel* (Philadelphia: Westminster Press, 1973), p. 13. Copyright © MCMLXXIII, The Westminster Press. Used by permission.
4. This view has been restated by Harold Lindsell's unfortunate book, *The Battle for the Bible* (Grand Rapids: Zondervan, 1976).
5. Walter Wink, *The Bible in Human Transformation* (Philadelphia: Fortress Press, 1973), p. 1.

2. The Liberation of Lazarus

1. This paragraph owes much to the observations by Fred B. Craddock's book on preaching, *As One Without Authority* (Enid, Oklahoma: Phillips University Press, 1971), chap. 1, especially pp. 12-14.
2. Hans W. Frei, *The Eclipse of Biblical Narrative* (New Haven: Yale University Press, 1974). See also my review in *Theology Today*, Winter, 1975.
3. Brevard S. Childs, *Biblical Theology in Crisis* (Philadelphia: Westminster Press, 1970).
4. There is an explosion of literature on structuralism and its import for exegesis. A good collection of essays was published in the April, 1974, issue of *Interpretation* (Vol. 28). See also the article by D. Robertson. "Literature, the Bible as," in *The Interpreter's Dictionary of the Bible* (Nashville: Abingdon, 1976), Supplementary Volume, pp. 547-51, and the extensive bibliography cited there.
5. L. E. Keck and G. M. Tucker, "Exegesis," *The Interpreter's Dictionary of the Bible* (Nashville: Abingdon, 1976), Supplementary Volume, pp. 296-303.

4. When Preaching Becomes Biblical

1. The *Gospel Parallels*, edited by B. H. Throckmorton and published by Thomas Nelson, uses the RSV. It is the English equivalent of Huck's

Synopse (published by the American Bible Society), which prints the Greek text. A more elaborate Greek "parallels" has been constructed by Kurt Aland, *Synopsis Quattuor Evangeliorum* (Stuttgart: Württembergische Bibelanstalt, 1964). It also includes John, and its listing of variant manuscript readings is much more complete. An English equivalent of Aland's edition is planned. The *Gospel Parallels* not only prints the Synoptic materials in parallel columns, but like Huck prints the lines in such a way that one can see at a glance precisely what words the three Gospels share and where they diverge. The student who color-codes this book constructs a permanent tool for his or her work. William Farmer has published a color-coded Greek "Parallels" called *Synopticon* (New York: Cambridge University Press, 1969).

2. *Proclamation Commentaries* began to appear in 1976. So far, studies of Matthew, Mark, Luke, John, and Hebrews-Revelation have been published. These are not running commentaries that treat the text verse by verse; rather they deal with overarching themes in order to help the preacher understand the books as wholes. My own contribution, *Paul*, will probably appear in 1978.

3. *The Good News According to Mark* and *The Good News According to Matthew* were published by John Knox Press in 1970 and 1975. Both translate German commentaries by Eduard Schweizer written for pastors.

4. For an instructive discussion of methods and problems, see J. Maxwell Miller's *Old Testament and the Historian* (Philadelphia: Fortress Press, 1976).

5. Rudolf Bultmann, *The History of the Synoptic Tradition* (New York: Harper, 1963,) pp. 150-63.

6. *A Future for the Historical Jesus* (Nashville: Abingdon, 1971). In the paragraphs that follow, I have extracted and paraphrased points stated more fully there.

7. Milan Machoveč, *A Marxist Looks at Jesus* (Philadelphia: Fortress Press, 1976).

5. To Be Specific: Three Sermons

I. *"Suppose We Count on God's Goodness"*

1. See also the comments on parables, pp. 136-37. I see no reason why a regular Sunday sermon in a parish could not, at some point, include some comments like these on the nature of parables.

2. This paragraph, and those that follow, are clear instances of incorporating anticipated responses to the text, as discussed on pp. 64-66.

3. Recall what was said about the importance of the plot for understanding a parable. This sermon attempts to adhere rigorously to the plot because every item in it is in place and helps to propel the meaning.

4. The offense created by Jesus is central to the possibility of preaching the historical Jesus, as outlined on pp. 134-35.

5. Note that the following concretions are not moralizing applications of the parable, but appropriations of its points as horizons of understanding and living. The hearers are not told what to do or think, but are given specific sketches of what appropriation of the parable implies. The invitation to accept the parable as an expression of truth is therefore tacit; it is a soft, not a hard sell.

6. Quoted from *God Is for Real, Man*, by Carl F. Burke (New York: Association Press, 1966), pp. 72-74.

II. "Jesus and Contemporary Heresy"

1. This sermon remains within the Johannine perspective. It does not emerge from the level of "what really happened" but from the level of John's distinctive way of portraying the meaning of Jesus' Passion (see pp. 124-33). Even if this sermon had been developed for a setting other than a university chapel, I would have called attention to the distinctive Johannine narrative, and to the nonhistorical portrayal of Pilate. Most congregations need not be shielded from such matters.

2. The allusion to John 3:19 should be clear. In the background of the sermon stands exegetical work on the distinctive Johannine understanding of light and darkness, "world," and of the frequent use of "the Jews" to represent the world's hostility to the revealer. John is not anti-Semitic. The sermon probably should have made this more explicit.

3. The order of service permitted me to read the Scripture at this point. Even if the story has been read before the sermon, or separated in time from it, I would have given it a setting. Far too frequently, the Scripture passage is read without any introduction (other than a pious remark), as if one could understand an extract from an argument or from a story in isolation from its context. Frequently the way Scripture is treated in the service suggests that the hearer is not really expected to understand what is read but merely to honor it.

4. At this point the sermon is deliberately "Johannine." That is, it probes the religious/theological reality that is embedded in the story. John's Gospel is not only a report of the revealing event of Jesus that occurred once upon a time, but an account designed to let that event keep on revealing. Because the text deals with Jesus and Pilate, it is appropriate to probe what Jesus discloses about political power. True, this is not the only thing the New Testament says about the subject, but to have rounded out the picture would have dulled John's point.

III. "Limited Resources, Unlimited Possibilities"

1. The order of service permitted me to delay reading the Scripture until this point. By introducing the Scripture in this way, the preacher abets its capacity to intersect the situation of the congregation. Notice that in this setting, the story functions as an "answer" to a problem that has been identified. (See comments on Scripture as occasional literature,

pp. 82-84.) Notice also that the introductory sentence points away from the miraculous, inviting the hearers to listen for something else, something not expected.

2. It is vital to respect the fact that the text is a story, not a theological argument. In preaching from stories, it is important to develop the sense of the plot, the dynamic of the story as a story, not as an allegorical code for timeless truths.

3. By using modern slogans to comment on the disciples in the story, the sermon suggests a link between those who are accosted by Jesus' words originally and those who are about to be accosted by them in the sermon. This link is made explicit two paragraphs later.

4. By getting "inside" the disciples' thinking, one can build into the sermon the dynamic analogous to the *diatribe* (see chap. 2). The story itself invites the preacher to develop the dynamic tension between Jesus and the disciples.

5. Shifting the focus of attention away from Jesus the miracle worker is congruent with Mark's own procedure. See pp. 94, 96; see also pp. 118-19.

6. Instead of moralizing—exhorting the hearers to do this or that—the appeal of the sermon is understated, relying on the hearer's imagination to make the necessary connections. Such a response is already "inside" the hearer; a moralizing application must be internalized, and runs the risk of being rejected. For comments on moralizing, see pp. 100-105.